Black Night at
Big Thunder Mountain

... ast in 1961, ... author of *Burning Your Own*, winner ... ...
Prize for Irish Literature, and *Fat Lad*, shortlisted
for the GPA Book Award. He has been writer in
residence at the Universities of East Anglia and
Cork. He has lived in Norwich, Manchester and
Cork, and is currently writer in residence at
Queen's University Belfast

Glenn Patterson

Black Night at Big Thunder Mountain

Minerva

A Minerva Paperback
BLACK NIGHT AT BIG THUNDER MOUNTAIN

First published in Great Britain 1995
by Chatto & Windus Limited
This Minerva edition published 1996
by Mandarin paperbacks
an imprint of Reed International Books Limited
Michelin House, 81 Fulham Road, London SW3 6RB
and Auckland, Melbourne, Singapore and Toronto

A CIP catalogue record for this title
is available from the British Library
ISBN 0 7493 9563 X

Typeset in 11 on 14 point Janson and Univers Bold
by Deltatype Ltd, Ellesmere Port
Printed in Great Britain by
BPC Paperbacks Ltd

For
Nessie and Phares Patterson,
my mother and father.

*Therefore they did set over them
taskmasters to afflict them with their burdens.
And they built for Pharaoh treasure cities,
Pithom and Raamses . . .*

Exodus 1: 11

2318

Sam still says there's a simple solution to this: Mort shows, that's it settled, everyone can go home. End of story.

Ilse and Raymond nod as freely as they are able. (You have to imagine them the way they are sitting, on a narrow mountain shelf, like bookends either side of Sam, who holds in his left hand the corners of the blanket that binds them to him and holds in his right a pistol cocked to reinforce the knot.) Sam has explained the whole thing more than once already tonight and each time they nod, but each time he feels there is something he has forgotten to say and has to go back to the beginning again; wherever the beginning happens to be at that moment, with Mort, or with the mud, or with the mountain itself.

Sam says from the moment he spotted the door lying in the mud this evening, in the no-man's-land between the compounds and the berm, he understood exactly what was required of him. He stripped to the waist and lay down flat on the duckboards, stretching out an arm until he had prised the door up on to its hinges. The mud underneath was a stippled mousse, perfectly rectangular, Sam says, like the face of an enormous unfired brick. He stepped down into it and began solemnly to anoint himself: face, neck, hair, chest, arms, whatever else he could get at. The mud hugged his calves (*sauce of dead things and dying things and ground-down things*) and clutched at the base of his thighs (*source of all that creeps and grows*). He clapped his back with clammy palms and felt it ooze out over his kidneys. Purifying.

A group of men in German border-guard parkas were watching him from the duckboards across the way. He called out to them.

"How you doing?"

They stared, expressionless, silent in the rain falling orange in the light of a passing truck. He rippled the surface with his fingers.

"Come on over," he said and sank to his knees. "The mud's fine."

The men spoke to each other in what sounded to Sam like Italian, shrugged, turned on their heels. Sam stood up.

"Hey, don't go. *Hey*. Do you know who I am?"

He whooped and threw himself back into the mire.

"Sam the frigging Mud Man!"

Sam says we are the earth-spread spawn of mud-diggers and mud-shifters, mud-shapers and mud-bakers.

Sam says that the mountain is a powerful place; its peaks are spires, its painted vaults holy shrines.

Sam says there is a bomb in the bag that he left on the track two yards from the ledge where he and Ilse and Raymond are sitting. He says if there's no sign of Mort by seven o'clock tomorrow morning he's going to blow him and them and the holy fucking mountain all to shit: *Boomph!*

Ilse and Raymond repeat the sound in the faintest of whispers, nodding their heads slower and slower, until they have nodded themselves into silent trances.

Boomph!

Sam, though, needs to keep talking. The mountain is alive with eyes just waiting for him to blink. Lights prowl its tunnels and caves. The world outside is a hum of tongues, talking about him. He glances at his wristwatch. Twenty after eleven. Shit. He taps his feet whistling "Love in an Elevator", then something he has forgotten the name of off *Surfer Rosa*, then stops, abruptly, detecting a disturbance in the sounds beyond the mountain: a low grumble (he thinks bikes at first and thinks what a wild way that would be for Mort to arrive, roaring in over the berm), a grumble which becomes a grunge and ends up a mechanical brawl (a frigging *rocket* maybe). . .

Something gives, a snap like the earth's crust cracking, the lights go out. This is it, Sam thinks, tightening his grip on the gun and drawing in closer to the rock face. Ilse and Raymond follow involuntarily, numbed extensions of himself. He waits, speeding but calm, ready for anything. But then the lights return and the noise starts up again and changes down through all the gears from brawl to grumble to gone and then there is once more only the hum of tongues.

Shit.

Sam takes the ends of the blanket in his gun hand and digs in his shirt with the other for the radio. He switches it on and the hum outside is instantly silenced.

"What's going on out there?"

"Sam," a voice comes back. "It's OK, don't worry. A glitch in one of the generators. Everything's under control."

"Never mind the generators," Sam says. "You've had four hours, I want to know, *what's going on?*"

"Sam," – always the same voice, says to call him Gary, but Sam is having none of it – "Sam, it's been a long time, you have got to realise we might not be able to find him at such short notice. Why don't you come on out and we can all wait together in the warm and the dry?"

Sam smacks his head, theatrically, with the heel of his hand, staggered by the transparency of the ploy. He thinks that for all their apparent reasonableness in dealing with him they are not yet taking this very seriously at all.

"I have to wait here. I can feel him trying to reach me. Somebody's stopping him getting through."

"Nobody's stopping anything, Sam. We're doing our best. All I'm saying is, it might not be possible."

"What do you mean, not possible?" Sam says.

His voice rises to a shout, then goes on rising. Ilse and Raymond resurface simultaneously, the words resound in their skulls, resound around the cavern, and out across the encircling moat of mud – as though the mountain itself had spoken – into every corner of the Magic Kingdom.

"This is fucking Disney. *Everything's* possible."

*

"These are the words of the Lord of Hosts, the God of Israel: to all the exiles whom I deported from Jerusalem to Babylon. Build houses and live in them, plant gardens and eat the produce; marry wives and rear families; choose wives for your sons and give your daughters to husbands, so that they may bear sons and daughters."

At seven twenty-five that morning, local time, a minibus was motoring, in light entirely of its own creation, along a country road in Marne-la-Vallée, east of Paris, radio tuned to the morning prayer from London.

"Increase there and do not dwindle away. Seek the welfare of any city to which I have exiled you and do not dwindle away. Seek the welfare of any city to which I have exiled you, and pray to the Lord for it; on its welfare, your welfare will depend."

In the minibus are sixteen Northern Irish labourers and tradesmen travelling in to work from their digs in a converted monastery south of Crécy-la-Chapelle. Two men sit up front with the driver, the remainder are packed in the back in unequal rows of six and seven, the spare man, jammed between his neighbour and the door, more out of his seat than in.

There are few houses to be seen. On either side the road falls away unbordered into dark flat fields. Sleet flurries dash against the windscreen like swarms of night insects. It is cold in the bus and black and silent. The men hug themselves for warmth. Only the driver appears to be fully awake.

"Living God, you have promised never to desert us. You go with your people into the exiles of their lives. When we are overwhelmed by the new and the foreign, give us your love which drives out fear so that we may serve the welfare of the community where we find ourselves. Help us to welcome strangers knowing that they are often your angels and messengers, coming to us in disguise."

A wan stripe appears unpromisingly along the horizon to the east. The driver lights a cigarette from the element in the dashboard. The man behind him coughs, without waking, the man beside *him* shifts his weight on to the other hip. The momentum continues along the uneven line, increasing in magnitude as it passes, so that the sixth man's giant sigh dislodges the seventh man altogether and tips him on his arse on the floor.

The seventh man doesn't even try to get up. Consciousness forms, a thin ice between him and the depths of sleep. He tells himself he's as well off where he is. His name is Raymond Black, he has only recently been moved to the monastery from Meaux and he isn't one to start a fuss. From the floor he sees twelve pairs of folded arms, twelve heads lolling over twelve shadowy chests. He sees roadside poplars ignite for a moment in the minibus's headlights, then turn to instant silver skeletons in their wake. After a few moments he lets his own head fall forward again, folding in on himself, back through the ice, dragging shards of World Service news beneath the surface with him.

Vukovar. A word like the crack and echo of a single rifle shot, drifting through smoke from which a building slowly emerges. . . A warehouse? Yes, on the edge of an anonymous Russian city. Inside, he knows, are six Red Army soldiers. They have held up the German advance for two days with only their rifle shots. The world is at war and Raymond Black is the narrator. He forms a sentence incorporating the words courage and terror. His voice is coming from inside the warehouse: a message, a mayday, an act of defiance. And then the transmission cuts out and he wakes.

The minibus is parked in a filling station forecourt, its engine and radio both silent. Instead a transistor is playing in the station shop. The reception is poor, swooping and soaring, from wavelength to wavelength, from speech to song, mixing the two into screech and babble. Ecstatic.

Vukovar. Raymond remembers at children's church in Belfast how he sang and clapped and shouted and the walls of Jericho came tumbling down. (He tries to remember Jericho's crime, but can't.) He remembers later, at school, on a page in his history book headed The Last Days of Rome, a picture of a Vandal tugging an old man's beard and the shame he felt every time he read the terse inscription: *Rome fell and was sacked.*

The driver gets back into the cab and fishes the docked cigarette from a sundae dish of butts Blu-tacked to the dashboard. The bus lurches out on to the road. The men lurch with it. There is a rumour doing the rounds that they are all going to be put on a month's notice at the end of the week. There have been no new starts for going on a fortnight as it is and some of the other contractors are already paying off their skilled men. It'll be all over by Christmas is the new catchphrase.

Raymond uses the door handle to pull himself up level with the window. Houses begin to appear with some regularity now at the side of the road; they clot into villages, the villages in turn into a small town. None makes any lasting impression on the darkness, but then at a certain point beyond the town the road dips for a moment and bends and when it rises again the sky has erupted into colour a mile or so distant. Lights stretch back as far as the eye can see, running off to the left and the right, clambering up the sides of buildings, silhouetting turrets and mountain peaks. The minibus finds itself in a flow of traffic which thickens and slows as more traffic joins at each new junction. Across the unveiled fields other roads can now be made out, drawing still more traffic in towards the centre. Buses, vans, lorries, taxis, private cars, motorbikes and pushbikes; and everywhere, from nowhere, groups of men, few of them white, walking. Hands slap on the side of the minibus, faces appear at the sleety windows mouthing words for lift and please.

Away and fuck! the driver says and holds the horn down with his fist. The men inside begin to come awake. They yawn, light cigarettes, look out over their shoulders at the acres of carparks they pass alongside, at the compounds with their national flags and own-language signs – little Italys and Belgiums and two kinds of Ireland – or squint through the wipers at the pink and blue castle and the stiff red fingers of Big Thunder Mountain.

"Are we past the Queen's Bridge yet?" some joker asks

and the men smile remembering other mornings closer to home.

Raymond smiles too.

The joker stops joking and leans forward.

"What are you smirking at, Black?" he says and twelve pairs of eyes all turn on Raymond, as the sleet thins to rain – as Vukovar falls – as the Euro Disney rush hour peaks and the minibus is waved through the gate and is lost among the lights and the mud and the clamour and the roar.

*

From seven o'clock to seven forty-five every morning except Sunday morning Ilse Klein cracks eggs in the Singer canteen. She cracks the eggs into a film of fat on a stainless steel hotplate, one metre long by half a metre wide, and drops the shells into the bucket which Rachid carries behind her. She never breaks a yolk. She fries the eggs in rows of ten. The whites flow together and bond, the unbroken yolks darken and subside. By the time she has reached the end of the fifth row, the eggs in the first row are cooked. She cuts them into squares with the edge of her spatula and lays them on the Pyrex plates that Rachid has set out for her along the serving hatch. In this way she cooks fifty eggs in fifteen minutes. She does this three times every morning, six mornings every week. Nine hundred eggs a week for more than four months and never once a broken yolk. Sometimes Pepe stands at her shoulder while she cracks the shells, trying just one time to put her off, but Ilse carries on as though he isn't there, moving always the same distance to the side into the space he has just stepped out of. Once Pepe asked her, *What do you do on Sundays when you have no eggs to cook for the men to eat?* and without pausing she broke the egg she was holding at that moment, threw back her head and drank down the contents, then tossed the shell into Rachid's

8

bucket and stepped one pace to the right. *Ouch!* Pepe made a face and limped off holding his hands between his thighs. The men on the other side of the hatch cheered. Pepe likes to set himself up in this way. Besides, Ilse is a good worker and he respects her. What Ilse does when she is not at the canteen is no concern of his, just so long as she is there in the morning at seven. She has a tiny Fiat he sees her drive off in in the evenings, but he has no idea where she drives to in it. All he knows about her is that the letter of reference she carried when she arrived came from Berlin. That does not surprise him. People turn up here from all over looking for work. And not just the usual types. It is the name of course, Disney. It is magical, even if you are only cracking eggs in a canteen for British workers or labouring all day in the rain and the mud and sharing ten showers between one hundred and twenty men in your lodgings, miles from anywhere.

At eight o'clock every morning Ilse Klein switches off her hotplate and drains the fat while Rachid clears the canteen tables. (Rachid is seventeen and speaks no English or German and only a little French; Ilse speaks no Spanish or Arabic; but they understand each other just fine.) Then they both go with Pepe and Imma, Pepe's daughter, to collect the vegetables for the midday meal. Sometimes Ilse has an hour or so free and then she can be seen in the town of Esbly shopping for herself or drinking coffee and reading a book. It is thought by some in Esbly, from the books she reads, that she is English, though others say her accent is German. She *is* known to have a problem with the veins at the back of her right leg which often necessitates the wearing of an elastic bandage. It is a small town and gossip is cheap entertainment.

It was in Esbly this morning that the strange thing befell her. She had just come out of the post office and was making towards the station, where she had left her car, when a

9

young man stepped up to her and placed his hand on her sleeve.

"I know you," he said and smiled.

Ilse recognised him at once, though his face was raw with cold this morning and the rain had made wet claws of his hair about his forehead. There was a time, not so long ago, when he had been a frequent visitor to the Singer canteen. So frequent, in fact, that Pepe had taken to referring to him as Ilse's American Friend, though he never once spoke to her directly and if anything, Ilse thought, showed more interest in Imma, who was after all closer to him in age than she was by almost twenty years.

She smiled back a little unsurely.

"Yes, from the canteen," she said, looking at the space on his blue anorak where his name tag should have been. "You're . . . ?"

"No." He shook his head. "You don't understand. I *know* you, Ilse Klein."

Ilse shrank inside her coat. The sound of her name in his mouth unnerved her, as though in uttering it he had transformed it into something no longer hers. His eyes too disturbed her, seeming one moment to implore her, the next to sneer. She excused herself and continued walking back to the car, quickening her step the further away she got from him, until finally, ludicrously, she was running. (They remarked on it in the shops. The woman with the German accent and the English novels, flying like the wind towards the station.) When she drove past the spot a minute later he was still standing there. His eyes were closed and his face was tilted up to the rain. Ilse accelerated away, but a kilometre or so beyond the town she eased her foot off the pedal, recalling something Pepe had told her the week before. Big fight, he'd said: inside the berm. *Your American Friend, he's in a lot of trouble.*

She had not paid it much attention at the time (with Pepe there were no little fights) and by next morning Pepe had found something else to amuse him and there were one hundred and fifty eggs to be cracked and Ilse had forgotten the conversation entirely. Thinking back now, though, she realised she had not seen the American Friend since. She thought of him standing alone in the rain. He was not very old at all. And to be in trouble and far from home . . . She stopped the car and rested her chin on the steering wheel a few moments, then turned around and drove back the way she had come.

She drove slowly along the town's transverse main streets, peering into the shops, but did not see him. At the station they told her that a train had just that minute gone up to Paris. The young American, she remembered then having noticed, had been carrying a heavy sack on his back. She wondered at her concern and laughed a little at herself, running around the French countryside like Mother Hen. Even so, it occurred to her to relate the meeting to Pepe, to make it into a story to entertain him; but only Rachid and Imma were in the canteen when she got back and once again she put the strange young man out of her head.

*

Raymond spent the morning with Nat Stanley painting stalactites up in Big Thunder Mountain. The two of them had worked together for a while over in Small World when Raymond was first taken on at the site. Then, Raymond couldn't get away from Nat quick enough. Nat was Saved (Touched some would have said) and every so often, sometimes in the middle of a sentence, he would clench his fists to his forehead and sing, as though it had just that moment occurred to him, *What a friend we have in Jesus. . .* And that was all. The same line, over and over, so that one guy who had been closeted with him for two days in Phantom Manor walked off the job saying he wasn't coming back till Nat learnt the rest of the words, or forgot the seven he already knew. Nat was not a popular man to work with. All the same, Raymond was not sorry to have been paired with him this morning. He was still feeling nervous after the incident in the minibus.

Not that it should have come as any great surprise.

He had been warned in the dinner queue one night last week that some fellas from Meaux were spreading stories about him and saying they were going to teach him a lesson. *I'd keep my head down the next few days, if I was you,* his informant said. Raymond ladled custard over his coconut sponge, said nothing. He had been keeping his head down for so long as it was he had begun to develop a permanent stoop.

At lunchtime he decided to give the canteen a miss and went instead for a walk with Nat to the souvenir shop. Nat had a week's leave coming up on Friday and a small army of nieces and nephews in Belfast counting down the days to his return. Raymond, who had opted to work through all the holidays due to him so far, had not had occasion to go to the shop before now.

Outside the mountain, the day had not amounted to much; the sky hung flat and low, a cold grey lid leaking rain. Men sheltered beneath the awnings of catering caravans parked along the perimeter road: French mainly, drinking coffee from miniature polystyrene cups. To the side of one caravan, tables had been improvised from cable spools turned on their ends and topped, optimistically, with sun umbrellas; beside another was a menu board, still proclaiming in pink paint (weeks after the second leg had wiped the result itself out) *Auxerre 2 Liverpool 0*. Flags clung to poles above portakabins and gateways, lank as dish-mops, indistinguishable.

For respite, Raymond and Nat took a shortcut through one of the scenery workshops, where sections of an enormous banyan tree had been spaced out in rows across the floor, painted, ready for assembly up on site. The whole rigid plantation was being tended by just one man, walking from section to section, checking the numbers tagged to each top branch against a list attached to his clipboard.

"Heaney!" Nat called to him.

The man looked up from his work at the two figures dripping water in the doorway.

"Well, Nat."

Heaney and Nat went way back. They had met as apprentices in Ford Autolite in Belfast and their paths had crossed at intervals since, in factories and firms once thriving now defunct. Their last job together before coming to France was fitting out a palace in Iraq.

Heaney indicated with his chin the world beyond the banyans.

"What would you say to Baghdad a day like that, Nat?"

Nat bunched his fists against his forehead, sang his line without registering it.

"Now you're talking," he said.

The Euro Disney shop was smaller than Raymond had expected, tucked away down a side road, opposite the security guards' headquarters and next to the resort's advance booking office. A pair of boots, swollen to twice their normal size with wet clay, had been left by the front door. Raymond saw their owner standing just inside, flicking through a rack of T-shirts, rubbing each sock-soled foot in turn against the backs of his legs. The other customers had kept their boots on, though they all handled the merchandise gingerly, trying not to get any of it dirty. Conversation was whispered, multilingual, and, judging from the accompanying gestures, composed almost entirely of exchange-rate calculations. Nat spent over 1200F in fifteen minutes. He bought stuffed toys and games for his nieces and nephews, key rings and ornaments for his brothers and sisters, a book for his father, a video for his mother, and for himself a baseball cap with *Euro Disney Opening Crew* emblazoned across the front.

Raymond, at the last minute, bought a 5F postcard showing an artist's impression of Frontierland and the Rivers of the Far West, with a grizzly bear, an American eagle, a gold prospector, and a moose looking in from the four corners and Big Thunder Mountain rising red in the centre.

The road from the shop back up to the mountain took Raymond and Nat across ground which, as the postcard prophesied, was soon to be submerged beneath millions of gallons of water. The imminent flooding of the site, the exact date of which was a source of constant argument among the workforce, had come to represent in all their minds the effective end of the first phase of building in Marne-la-Vallée, and with it most of their jobs. Their disappointment, though, was tempered by a daily-growing sense of pride in what they would be leaving behind. Because none of them were in any doubt that something extraordinary had happened here these last few months, something that could not simply be reckoned in terms of the millions spent or the tens of thousands employed. Nor was it the sort of thing that they could easily talk about when they got home, at least not without making it into some sort of wisecrack. For the difference, they all knew, between this and any other work they had ever done lay, in the end, with the character whose face smiled down on them at all hours of the working day – whose portrait had been executed in flowers at the entrance to Main Street USA – whose ears, attached to black skullcaps, visiting dignitaries ritually donned – and who posed, dressed like the men themselves in dungarees, on the Opening Crew caps and sweatshirts so many of them sported.

Mickey Mouse was no joke inside the Euro Disney berm. He was what held it all together. The castle, the mountain, the labyrinth, the fort, the riverboats and railroads, the town square, the *Bazar*, Autopia and Videopolis, the Past and the Future. He was as real as royalty.

As Nat and Raymond were crossing the isthmus of planks leading out to the mountain they saw a workman standing in a fold near the base, urinating. His piss flowed back between his legs and on to the mud, mingling with puddles turned sulphur and blood-orange by the paint washed down from the manmade summits.

"Hallian," Nat said, and turned his head away.

Later in the afternoon, while Nat was down in the paint storeroom making tea, Raymond took a pen from his overall pocket and smoothing out the postcard on his thigh began to write:

Dear Stephanie. Well how's this for a surprise? Don't worry, I didn't dig right the way across! (Not quite anyway.) Well, I bet you you'll never guess where I'm sitting writing this? Right in the middle of that big mountain you can see on the front there! No kidding – it's a "True Bill". ("True WHAT?" says you. Ask your mum.) Hard to believe you could make something like that out of just steel and cement, eh? Well, I hope you are well, Stephie, as I am here. How is school and what have you? Will write longer when I have the time. Lots of Love, Daddy R.

He looked over what he had written, trying to imagine it through Stephanie's eyes. He was nearly sorry he had started. Writing to his daughter always left him wishing he had said something more, or nothing at all.

PS Just thinking how much you'd like it here – do you remember the time we went to see the "101 Dalmatians"!

The day after her eighth birthday. He had picked her up from May's mother's in Craigavon. Mrs Clark said he had only missed May herself by a couple of minutes. Stephanie was shy with him to start with. She had a new doll – Disco Sindy – and sat with her eyes lowered all the while they were in the house, brushing out its long silvery hair with a turquoise comb. The doll's shoes, a glittery red, were an almost perfect match for the ones May was wearing in the photo on Mrs Clark's mantelpiece. May and a girlfriend toasting the camera; happy.

Even on the bus into Belfast Stephanie wouldn't look at him straight, but answered his ever more desperate questions with little jerky nods, or big sweeping shakes of her head. Only in the picture house itself did the day begin to change. Stephanie sat through the film transfixed and when the tension got too much for her to bear she slipped her hand into his on the arm rest.

"It'll be all right," he told her. "Wait till you see."

Her face then when she did finally turn her head was just eyes, looking at her father.

Raymond had at long last found a job that week down at the shipyard, cleaning the tanks on car ferries that were in for repair: sick-making work, but there was nothing else in Belfast then. He was still there the following year when the letter arrived from May to say she was getting married and taking Stephanie to New Zealand. The next week Raymond boarded the ferry he had just finished cleaning and crossed the water to Scotland. It was many months before he heard, from a friend who had seen her in Belfast, that May hadn't emigrated after all, but it was too late for him by that stage: once he had started on his plan to build a new life for himself he couldn't stop. He hadn't been back to Belfast since.

Raymond was putting the card back in his pocket when Nat appeared at the top of the stairs carrying the two teas, smiling.

"I was speaking to a young lad downstairs," he said, handing Raymond a cup, "says he knows a friend of yours."

Raymond blew sawdust from the surface of his tea and sipped.

"What's this now he said you called him? Somebody Thompson."

Raymond stopped sipping.

"Wally, was it?" Nat mumbled.

"Ollie."

"*Ollie.*" Nat nodded. "Well, the young lad downstairs says you're to tell Ollie Thompson hello from him next time you see him."

Nat beamed his satisfaction at having delivered the message. Raymond sat in silence.

"Is there something the matter?" Nat asked.

Raymond watched the sawdust regroup in the centre of his cup.

"Ollie Thompson's been dead for years," he said.

"Oh, no."

Nat's beaming face imploded. People perplexed him. He couldn't imagine why anyone would ask a man to say hello to a dead pal, let alone involve him in it.

"I'm sorry. I didn't know."

He stood up and began inspecting the stalactites, then

suddenly clenched his fists to his head.

"What a friend we have in Jesus," he sang into his wrists, and when that didn't console him, sang it again until it did.

"What a friend we have in Jesus."

*

Sam hadn't slept more than a couple of minutes at a stretch for going on seventy-two hours. The past two days he had stayed in his hotel room in Château Rouge, ingesting amphetamine, waiting for a signal. He listened to the radio, watched the television, had as many papers ordered up as the quarter's news sellers could send him – some in languages he could barely identify never mind translate – and read them all regardless, cover to cover. He read, in addition, instructions on wrappers, labels on clothes, the notices pinned to the back of his door. All he was looking for was the right word.

Sometimes he simply lay on the bed, sifting the sounds coming in at his window. Late at night there were voices raised in the street below and sirens in the distance. At the end of the sirens, he thought, things were breaking down. He plotted their blue trails as they criss-crossed the city until it seemed as though they must have the whole of Paris stitched up: lying on the bed in his coat and shoes, bag ready by his side, gun loaded in his pocket.

He could not say for certain who it was in the end had convinced him of the need to buy a gun. The events and faces of the previous fortnight had all run together. There was the Frenchman on the Métro, drunkenly pulling an invisible trigger at his temple, the anarchists he had talked with at Les Halles, saying to him over and over in English, *Anything you want, you understand, anything*; there was the sad American expatriate art dealer, who had wanted to take him home to his bank vault in the 5th, appalled to hear where he had been wandering that week, and who told him he never went anywhere in the city unarmed; the Arab kids out at la Caravelle, showing him the knife scars they carried from racist attacks, who told him these days neither did they; there was Guillaume, there was Aimée. . . But perhaps it was none of these. There had been tens of other encounters. Dealers had been queuing to feed him speed, just to hear him tell his story. He was the man who had deserted Disney, he was a celebrity.

Somewhere along the line, though, he had begun to be very afraid, even of those who had been his companions of late. He was talking too much to too many people. He switched hotels again and from then on maintained his vigil alone, well clear of the street. Waiting for the word to act. Shortly after seven-thirty this morning, the third morning, he stood up abruptly, switched off the television and the radio and waded through the papers to the door.

He knew nothing of Ilse Klein's mornings off in Esbly. Meeting her was to that extent unplanned, though Sam was no believer in chance and merely accepted this as further proof that his instincts were good and that what he was doing was right. Coincidences of this sort were pearls he collected and strung together into flawless ropes. He felt, as he had first felt when he saw her in Pigalle three nights before, satisfied that things were at last beginning to work themselves out through him. Even so he nearly blew it in his excitement by going up to her and talking right there in the street. After she had gone he had forced himself into a minute's meditation. At times like this his mind seemed to inhabit a barren icy plateau. Time was suspended there. He saw and heard nothing, but he knew that whatever step he took next would be the right one.

They would still be on the lookout for him at the site, though perhaps not so assiduously as a few days before. He sat out the morning on a tree stump in parkland overlooking the river. He had paused as he turned off the street to count the names picked out in gold on the granite war memorial. He tried to make them tally with his estimate of the town's total population, but the numbers did not add up, at least not according to any equation of suffering he understood. This was slaughter on a Biblical scale. This was visiting on to the third and fourth generation. This was Europe. Someone had ditched a bunch of flowers in a trashcan he passed along the way and he had retrieved a couple for himself. Tiger-lilies. Sitting on the tree stump he removed their petals one by one, separating the anthers from the filaments, paring the stems into strips with his nails, expecting at any moment to find himself holding in his hand the vital element that had sent them shooting from their bulbs to burst above the earth like fabulous fireworks. Rooks gathered on the branches over-head, watching him. Sam stared back at them. Traffic passed on the wet road. Time passed. The rooks lifted off. When Sam looked down again his hands were wet and stained green. The remains of the flowers lay scattered at his feet. He moved the pieces around with his toe, making patterns. The rooks lit again on the bare trees, swaying in the wind like black pennants waving.

Night was already falling and the traffic was beginning to congest the exit roads by the time he came in sight of Euro Disney. He had walked the first three kilometres from Esbly in what seemed minutes, then stopped, suddenly aware of the straps of his sack cutting into his shoulders. He had forgotten about the sack. He had forgotten almost every-thing in his haste to get there except the act of walking itself.

A van was drawn up on the grass verge twenty yards ahead with its hazard lights flashing. There was something written across the rear doors in Greek script and repeated in the regular alphabet in brackets underneath. Before Sam could read any of it, though, one whole side was erased by a man stepping down from the back swinging a wheel out before him. Another man appeared now from the front of the van and began jacking it up.

"Need any help?" Sam asked.

The men glanced round, startled, uncomprehending.

"Help?" Sam said again and pointed at the wheel.

The man with the jack smiled but shook his head. Actually they were both pretty big guys. There wasn't much they couldn't have done without Sam's assistance. He watched them, hunched over their work, roll away the old wheel, position the spare against the axle and tighten the nuts. As the van was being lowered again he caught a glimpse through the side window of camera boxes and lighting equipment.

"TV?" he asked.

The Greeks looked at each other and laughed. Sam laughed along with them. So he was stating the obvious. What did he care? He pointed towards the distant lights.

"You driving to *Disney*?"

The taller of the two replied to Sam as slowly in Greek as Sam had spoken to them in English, nodding his head in truncated translation, *Yes*. He stowed the jack and the dud wheel in the back of the van then held the door open. *You come also?* he asked and made a mock bow as Sam took up his offer of a ride and climbed on board. His friend was already installed in the passenger seat, biting on his thumb, shoulders shaking with suppressed laughter. Sam laughed even harder. What did he care, so long as he got there?

Even at that late stage, though, he had no clear idea of what he would do once he was inside the main gate. Now that everything had been set in motion he was simply following signs, acting as the moment directed. So when the van became stuck in traffic outside the Pizzarotti yard, the

Pizzarotti yard seemed as good a place as any to ask to be set down. The Greeks took next to no notice of his leaving. The guy in the passenger seat had his personal camera out and was snapping all round him, though it was now more or less completely dark and out here there was nothing to see, only rain and mud and men and the back of the truck up ahead. Ad-hoc traffic cops blasted away on their whistles at busy intersections and were answered on all sides by horns and for minutes at a time nothing moved.

Sam kept well in to the side of the road, then abandoned it altogether for the lanes and alleys that had grown up between the company lots. Some of these had names scrawled on bits of wood stuck in the ground. O'Connell Street, Sauchiehall Street, Scheiss Strasse, Piccadilly Circus. At one point he came close to the road again, straying without realising into the frame of the Greek cameraman, and was caught for an instant in a freakish shaft of light between two chemical toilets, though, whether it was the angle of this light or the speed with which the composition came together, the Greek failed to recognise him as the man he had had in the back of his van just a few minutes before. He fired off one shot, but somebody else walked across it, and when he attempted a second the trigger resisted the pressure of his finger – film out. By the time he had changed rolls the moment, and the subject, had gone.

Sam in fact had spotted a safety helmet, split clean in two, behind one of the toilets. For a few moments he was completely engrossed by it. He picked up the two halves and walked with them in his hands four or five steps, tilting his face up towards the rain and letting his eyes slowly close.

What is this?

He opened his eyes. Two halves of a safety helmet. He threw them aside, then turning saw a door lying flat in the mud a few yards to his right.

Ilse Klein was shutting the Singer canteen when she saw the face at the window.

"Closed," she said.

The face moved along the darkness to the door. Rapraprap. Ilse Klein checked her watch against the canteen clock. Everyone else had already left for the night.

"*Fermé*," she said. "*Geschlossen*: Time to go home."

She secured the shutter over the counter and pocketed the key. There was another knock. The wind threw fistfuls of rain against the glass. The face looked in at her. Mud up to the eyeballs. Ilse sighed.

"All right," she said. "A coffee only. But quick."

She opened the door.

Why? She just did. All her life, she *just did*. Door closed, door open, now what?

*

Quigley and Mullan (who are Quigley and Mullan? Belfast skinheads in possession of passports, loopers, headers, space cadets), Quigley and Mullen hadn't a *fucking clue* what it was your man Black was supposed to have done that everybody was talking about. Nobody told Quigley and Mullan *fucking anything*. But do you know what? Quigley and Mullan *didn't give a fuck*. They didn't like Inspector Dick anyway. (Inspector Dick was Quigley and Mullan's name for your man, because of the way he walked about the place all hunched up, like he was trying to see down his own kacks.) Anyway, they were bored *fucking shitless* today. They were skiving off down at Liberty Arcade making nothing look like something, hoping they could string it out till six, when they thought of the gag.

Know your man. . . Know that wee cupboard up in the

mountain. . . Know has all them wires and all in it. . .
Know if we were to get the hold of the key. . .

Quigley and Mullan pulled a gawky gub at each other.
That'd fucking harden him.

*

Raymond had stayed on in the mountain after Nat Stanley
left, tidying up, trying his best to miss the first two buses
back to the monastery. He knew that on a dirty night like this
most of the men would leave as early as they could. On a
dirty night like this all anyone wanted to do was to eat,
shower, and try to sleep through the alien braying of the
monastery geese. The ground floor of the mountain was all
but deserted when he finally came down to clean his
brushes. Raymond released the breath he hadn't until then
even known he was holding: the last bus would be empty
too.

"Hi, mister."

A young lad wearing the company overalls, with a five
o'clock shadow for a hairstyle, was waving to him from the
doorway of one of the storage cupboards.

"Give us a hand there a minute, would you?"

Raymond vaguely knew the young lad to see. There were
usually two of them knocked about together. They had come
over in the last big intake about three weeks before. Couldn't
have been more than a few months out of school the pair of
them.

"Sure," he said, though in fact he wasn't entirely. But
then what else was he going to say? Besides, he still had over
a quarter of an hour to get to the pick-up point. He followed
the teenager into the cupboard. The name Quigley was
stencilled in white on the yoke of his donkey jacket and
running down from the U were the outlines of two more
letters, capital tee, capital aitch, which had recently been

24

picked off. Up The Hoods. Belfast's only ecumenical graffiti. The Hoods, a chaplain once suggested to Raymond, were what the men in masks, Catholic and Protestant, had bequeathed to their city.

"What is it?" Raymond asked.

"Here," said Quigley, indicating the ground.

Raymond stooped lower to see what he was pointing to. Up against the back wall a mound of something or other lay draped with a blanket. Raymond took a cautious step forward. Then *BLEH!* the blanket was thrown back and another skinhead, Quigley's mate, leapt up howling, demented. Raymond recoiled, but Quigley had moved in behind him and shoved him forward again, so that he stumbled head first into the blanket.

He took a couple of kicks as he went over, nothing serious, but by the time he fought his way out of the tangle, the room was in darkness and Quigley and his accomplice were gone.

"Harden you."

He didn't bother trying the door handle. He didn't even bother to shout. As soon as he heard the key turn in the lock, he knew it was out of his hands anyway. All the old feelings of powerlessness, reborn in an instant.

He groped along the walls till he found the light switch, then wrapped himself in the blanket his assailants had pulled over his head and sat down on a paint tin beneath the bare bulb to wait. He waited maybe twenty minutes or half an hour. Maybe more. He had no watch. Somewhere out there men were still working. This was another sensation he remembered, the world going on as though you weren't there, coming at you through your ears alone. Like a chick in an egg in a nest up a tree, the world at first was a puzzle in four dimensions to you. Given time, though, your hearing developed new heights and depths, your ears became as precise as slide-rules.

But he was out of practice and knew only that for twenty minutes or half an hour, maybe more, this evening no one came into the mountain.

Then all at once a man with an American accent, speaking from somewhere close at hand, said, quite distinctly, and as though arriving at a decision, *This is the place.* An odd sort of voice, though Raymond paused only a fraction of a second before running down the room and throwing himself on the door.

"Help!" he shouted. "Let me out."

His cry echoed briefly, then died, and there was silence.

"Over here! In the storeroom!"

He pounded the door still harder, then stood back, expectant. But the silence seemed only to deepen. He was confused, then confusion turned to fear. He withdrew to the rear of the storeroom and slid down the wall. He began to wonder whether this wasn't all part of the lesson the fellas from Meaux had wanted to teach him. But that was ridiculous; it was ten miles to Meaux, the buses would be long gone by now, and nobody had ever been known to miss the buses if they could possibly help it. He sat a moment longer then walked back to the door and shouted a third time.

"Please. Over here! I'm locked in."

And now at last his calls were heeded. Footsteps approached, hesitated, came on towards the door.

"Yes!" Raymond shouted his encouragement. "In here."

A hand began warily to turn the key.

"Thank you," he was saying, as the door swung open. "You saved me."

His liberator, unexpectedly, was a woman, about the same age as he was. Her eyes, on a level with his own, were wide with fright.

"It's all right," Raymond said, and then he saw over her shoulder the other eyes, staring, white, from the appalling

26

mudpack of the young man's face, and saw too the gun pointing at his own forehead from the flaking muddied fist.

*

"Who are you?"

The man in the doorway with the plaid blanket draped round his shoulders moved his mouth in answer to Sam's question, but made no sound. The look on his face, though, Sam thought, beyond the instant of surprise, was that this was no more than he had been expecting; and indeed he told himself that this was exactly where he would have expected to find *Raymond Black* – he finally managed to get his name out – even though he didn't know until he had Ilse Klein unlock the door who or what he was looking for.

(Doors, doors, doors. The rope grew stronger. Pearl after pearl after pearl.)

2333

All is calm again inside the mountain. Slow beams illuminate the interior at irregular intervals. Outside the generators grumble.

Sam *still* says there's a simple solution to this. Ilse and Raymond nod without knowing, repeating deep within their stunning: *Mort shows, that's it settled. End of story.*

The end though is only half of it.

The Vietnam body count the day Sam was born was eighty-five. Tom entered the figure as always in red in his diary then wrote below it, shakily, in black: *Sam arrived today. A boy.*

Sam was Sam before he was a sex. Sam was Sam to reclaim the name from the uncle whose air force was obliterating hamlets around the 20th Parallel the night he was conceived; *Sam* to defy the cops who had bludgeoned his parents out of Elysian Park, while he was still a thing more mathematical than physical in Holly's belly, the day the camel's back was broken.

Sam's parents were twenty-three, and eight months married, when, in the late summer of the year that they had even then begun to think of as *One*, they fled the City of Angels – baton-bruises ripening as they drove – and took the desert freeway east. When their journey ended, ten days later, they were parked before a wood-framed house on the other side of the continent, half a mile back from US Route 1 – twenty miles south of Bangor, Maine – in the lee of a hill overlooking Penobscot Bay. In the sixteenth century, French and English navigators had been enticed up the river that fed into this bay by tales of the fabulous city of

Norumbega that was believed to lie along its banks (and where, in true sixteenth-century-fabulous-city hyperbole, even the dog turds were diamonds), and were disappointed, to say the very least, when their explorations yielded only scattered huts covered with skins. But fabulous cities were the very things most of the people who turned up at this house had, like Tom and Holly, moved *downeast* to escape and they claimed instead spiritual kinship with the people whose way of life those first Europeans had so scorned: the Wabanaki Indians – "the dwellers at the sunrise" – the Dawnlanders.

The commune had been founded by a friend of Tom's from UCLA, a theology major named Jennifer, who had suddenly turned on a couple of summers back, phoned her parents from their holiday home in Maine and announced that she was confiscating it as a protest against privilege and throwing it open to the People. Her parents, of course, went apeshit. They threatened Jennifer with lawyers, blamed her lover (a *fortune-teller* – HA! – who had changed her name from Diane to Jen in homage) for corrupting her, blamed the occult – *blamed Bob Dylan* – for corrupting her lover, blamed just about everyone and everything they could think of, and in the fullness of time got around to blaming each other, so that when they did in fact go to law it was not to evict their daughter but to file for a divorce so huge and complex they were still caught up in its financial labyrinth many, many months later.

At the summer house, meanwhile, the People came and went: students, teachers, mystics, freaks, hippies, heads, and out-and-out bums; refugees from America Incorporated. Beans and vegetables were planted on the steep hillside at the back of the house, goats and chickens grazed and grubbed in large pens on either side of it. Crazy-coloured outhouses were added – a tepee was erected for a time. The words New Dawnland appeared painted in purple on the mailbox and, in the same hand, above the front door, the legend *Sous les pavés, la plage*. Wind-borne sand scoured the porch planks, like the fall-out from the earth-turning *événements* (for, they were in no doubt, the earth *was* turned around) across the Atlantic.

Tom and Holly were received like true family. The car that had brought them there gave out the night they arrived and never started again. They sold it to a wrecker's yard and, for no good reason they could think of, save that they couldn't think of a reason why not to, they bought a wheel on which Holly began, untutored, to throw pots: weird eruptions of red clay which Tom decorated with patterns of his own devising, leaving the house alone in the mornings to sit, cross-legged, on a boulder at the top of the hill and paint.

The country round about was dotted with these boulders, as though to keep the thin fields anchored to the hillsides. Tom was reminded of the dough pellets his mother had used to stop piecrusts rising in the oven. The memory disturbed him, as his memories of home often did these days. Viewed from here, in fact, his entire childhood seemed to have been conducted under a deadening pall of smoke, inside the house as well as out: smoke from the steel plant across the highway from his front yard, smoke from the three packs a day, minimum, his parents each managed to work their way through, sitting up half the night if need be, smoking as they drank – and did most other things: to excess – as though it was a patriotic duty. They were zombies, his parents; LA, their wonderful consumer society, had eaten up their hearts. He did not want that for his child.

Holly grew with Sam all through the fall and the hard Maine winter, and, as she grew, the balance of the commune began subtly, even hormonally, to change. (Jen, Jennifer's fortune-teller lover, claimed to have stopped menstruating.) There had never been a baby born at New Dawnland before. Little by little, Holly became the object of its collective days, wrapped around and protected by it, as if by an aura, an invisible amnion. At times, then, the world seemed to her recast entirely, infinite circles centred on her and the baby turning and turning inside her, like a cramped question mark awaiting issue.

Even the goats, diligently converting hay to milk for her to drink, and the frenetic hens did their bit.

The baby finally arrived, two weeks earlier than expected, on a Monday evening in late April. Jennifer swore that Jen felt the first contraction all the way up at the Canadian border, where they had driven in their little Volkswagen Bug in the hope of hearing a member of the Deserters' Committee speak. Just outside of Fort Kent, Jen gave a grunt like a poleaxed pig and slumped against the passenger door. Jennifer pulled over on to the shoulder. *Sam?* she asked, and when Jen nodded, weakly, swung the car right around and didn't stop till she had brought it, an hour after dark, skidding into the yard of New Dawnland.

The birth was already in progress. The whole house had shifted into delivery mode. Tom had retreated back against the bedroom wall, where he remained throughout the rest of the labour, stunned into silence by the ferociousness with which the two bodies fought to be free of one another – the bloody physics of force, mass and motion, brought to a climax by a double-headed scream as the baby finally broke through into terrifying free-fall.

S – A – A – A – M!

*

But maybe the beginning for Sam lies much further back. Then how about this, the ultimate in hesitant starts:

Ur.

(For centuries, perhaps, a clabber of huts on an island in a river till

Ziggurat! – a turning point: base earth aspires to heaven – Ur becomes urban. The pattern sets.)

Maybe.

*

69, the yin and yang year, the year with sex written all over it, turned a stark 70 three weeks prematurely at Altamont. New Dawnland was in confusion. The Sixties had been around for as long as anyone there could remember, so that their Fifties' selves seemed separated from them by something more profound than time. Sam teetered through the opening months of the new decade as though infected by the uncertainty of the grown-ups around him, then, impatient for a lead perhaps, took off on his own one day and ran headlong into it, hands waving, chin bearded with his happy drools.

Once started there was no holding him. The only child in a community of adults, he discovered the places only a child could know. Gaps and cracks were to him wide-open windows of opportunity. He quested in cupboards and under stairs with an unerring sense for where life was. Movement of any sort fascinated him, shadows, ripples on water; quick as a cat, he caught bugs barehanded and squatted with them, studying their undersides, the axle and struggling feet that strove to drive the sleek shells forward.

The house echoed to the sound of his name. Only Jen, though, seemed able regularly to find him out. She would crawl into his dirt kingdoms sometimes and place a finger on her lips, then sit with her arms locked round her knees and watch him play. Sam played as well as he was able, being watched.

There were house meetings now almost daily. Sam fell asleep in Holly's arms and woke, hours later, on a pillow at her feet to find the talking still going on. He clambered over legs, touched the faces of the speakers, poking his fingers into the wet holes of their mouths, trying to catch the words they spoke; they moved his hand away patiently, jiggled him in their laps. He saw the arguments for how to respond to the changing times from all angles without understanding a word of them and opening his hands in the shelter of the talking chins was disappointed to find that, for all the enormous sounds, he held nothing.

His father had a thin red beard which he would separate into three distinct strands with his forefinger and thumb while he listened then muss up into one again before he started to reply. He was quiet around Sam, as though not quite sure how to address him. Sam put his little face to his father's big one. *Tom*, he said.

In the fall of his second year ducks gathered on the pond a little way inland from the commune. For weeks the evenings were filled with their bleat and blare. Tom and Holly walked there some nights with their son. They watched the birds winging in from their duck-days upstate, corrugating the dull steel water as they landed. Loose individuals skated the periphery, their wake as long as the sorrows they proclaimed. Mornings found them a silent huddle in the middle of the pond, a wrack of down buffeted by the winds edging daily closer to true north. They pulled their necks in, narrowed their eyes to black-lidded slits and submitted to having their feathers rummaged through. Tom and Holly held on to each other.

Then, *warumph!* – with the suddenness of a fire igniting, the ducks were gone. Sam was with Holly when he saw the sky begin to billow with them. Wave after wave passed the bottom of the vegetable garden, utterly transformed by their purpose.

His mother held his hand tight, tight, laughing.

"Oh, Sam," she was saying. "Look at them."

Not long after, Tom and Holly moved out of New Dawnland and rented a trailer on the edge of the county seat two miles to the south. Tom took what work he could find, apple-picking on outlying farms, or helping at the harbour where lobster fishermen landed their pots. For some months when things were particularly tough he worked in a chicken processing plant. In the evenings, though, he still painted with his trademark wisps the pots Holly had thrown with increasing skill and fired in their home-made wood kiln.

There was a hardware store downtown where they shopped for their materials and where they sometimes managed to sell a finished pot or two. On the counter was a sign saying *Bowman – Cutting Keys for Seven Generations*, and below this was a board on which were mounted samples of the store's wares in a long line, the keys on the left massive and black, like great clanking musical notes, turning silvery as you moved to the right, shortening like the strings inside a piano, so that the last key – no thicker than a nickel, no longer than the top joint of a child's little finger – would have denoted a sound so high and light its being would seem instantly the echo of its having once been.

Sam was fascinated by this display and wanted to know what each of the keys was for. The seventh Mr Bowman would follow the direction of the child's finger.

"This key here? This is the key that unlocks the Jell-O safe," he might say, or: "That opens the drawer with the answer to the question of who started the battle of the sexes."

One afternoon, when Sam was in the store with his parents, Mr Bowman brought him through to the back room and lifted him up on to a stool beside a table on which stood a small oval box. Mr Bowman produced a key that was an exact match of the smallest key on the counter display. He slipped it into a lock which had appeared till then no more than a scratch in the decorative enamel. The sound of the key turning was the sound of morning eyelids parting.

"What do you reckon it is?" Mr Bowman asked, pausing with his hand on the key.

Sam shrugged, the word purple suggested itself. Mr Bowman waited a second longer then raised the lid. Sam jumped back on the stool as the figure of a man in a harlequin suit tumbled head first out of the box, springing up off his hands into a back-arching somersault, his paper-thin body rippling, landing on his feet and instantly leaping forward on to his hands and somersaulting again. He did this five times in all, leaning always a little to the left, so that he went into the fifth somersault having come full circle and arrived at the other end of the box. His face seemed carved out of blue eggshell, his mouth was a doll's red kiss. He launched himself forward, his feet struck the box's wooden floor and the rest of his body followed as if gathering itself for another leap when Mr Bowman blinked the lid shut again.

"What do you think of that?"

What Sam thought was that he would have traded all the purple in the world for that oval box and the little key to open and animate it.

Footsteps on the concrete overhead. Sam looks at his watch and sees it is a minute to midnight. He listens. There are other sounds outside besides the footsteps: vehicles continue to arrive at the Mining Company, where Gary and the cops and whoever else is out there have established their incident management headquarters; there are, now and then, voices raised; there is still the rain. Yet above it all he can hear quite clearly the ticking of his watch. He follows it, attentive to the timbre of every passing second. Each one is as unique as an individual voice.

He loves the sound this minute makes.

Ever since he was a child he has been aware of the peculiar properties of certain moments of time. Once, when he was six, he drove with his parents to Jennifer and Jen's house, the house where he was born (though he remembered then only this from that time: *feet* in the kitchen, loaves as big as pumpkins). for Jen's special birthday and was perplexed to count only seven candles on her cake. He asked Jen where the rest of the candles were, but she told him seven was the right number. (For a long time when he tried to call Jen to mind all he got was Jennifer. Jennifer's mannerisms, Jennifer's expressions, Jennifer's changing hairstyles. The two of them even dressed alike, their matching jean shirts fading in harmony. The only difference was that Jen sometimes had to wear dark glasses indoors, something to do, Sam guessed, with the hours she spent peering into the future. It must have hurt her eyes.)

"Don't you know what *date* it is?" she asked him.

Sam didn't. His life was still divided pretty much into day-time and night-time, in school and out of school. Even his own birthday was something of a recurring surprise. Jen handed him the calendar from on top of the refrigerator. It was the sort that had a leaf you tore off for each day, so that at the end of the year all you were left with was a bunch of dangling stubs.

"Well?" she said and made him read out the date.

"Sunday February 29."

Jen was a leap-year baby, and leap-year babies, she told Sam, only had a real birthday one year in every four. Sam wanted to know what happened to her birthday all the other years. Jen brought her finger and thumb close together in front of his nose, so close that a little flesh-coloured bubble appeared bridging the gap between them.

"It shrinks," she whispered (Jennifer's smell of goats and hens), "way, way down to this."

Long after he had tired of trying to make the link appear between his own finger and thumb Sam still had this extra day running around his head. As the years passed and he grew more familiar with calendar time he learnt to look out for the approach of February and willed himself not to sleep on the last night, lying in bed, watching through the jolt and sag of embattled wakefulness the clock tick down towards midnight. Always at a certain point his mind would clear and he would enter into a heightened state of alertness. The clock seemed to glow right in his face. His heart beat faster and faster as finally the second hand came round to marry the other hands together. An arrow, pointing: *in there*, it said, in that frozen instant, neither one thing nor the other, an extra day was squeezed. In his imagination it was a bright room opening up at the end of a narrow corridor and he dreamed in those days tantalising dreams that were sometimes part nightmare (but in a way that you knew they *were* only nightmares) of running along this corridor without ever reaching the end. Over time the room grew and grew until it had expanded almost into another world, where he imagined everything in this world could be turned on its head, where what went up, perhaps, did not have to come down, and where there was, sometimes, if you wanted it, smoke without fire. (When, at the beginning of the next leap year, he discovered that Jen had disappeared once and for all he was secretly convinced that was where she had gone.) Experimenting further, he found that if he squeezed his eyes shut tight and held his breath, stopping his ears, he could make the moment last longer. But eventually, of course, he would have to breathe out and straight away he would hear the second hand racing ahead, *tut*, *tut*, *tut* (there was no sound more indifferent than the sound of the first seconds on the other side of midnight), and Jen's day, his entire fantasy world, was wiped clean away.

Still, it was addictive. He began to wonder whether these chinks existed elsewhere, these elongated instants when time seemed stretched so thin that other possible worlds could be glimpsed underneath. He was sure it was because one of Jen's years had to cover four of everybody else's that she was able to see through time the way she did. Gradually he came to the conclusion – long before he came by the words to express it – that all midnights possessed this quality in some degree, the hands of the clock becoming sluggish and reluctant in the approach, as though the responsibility of starting another day was too onerous. And when at last they did meet it seemed sometimes that they would never part, or would fall back together rather than break their embrace and move forward alone.

*

Sam listens tonight to the seconds passing, slowing as the hands come together. Three in one. They cling. The silence is almost bottomless, almost unbearable.

0000.01

Tut. The second hand twitches, but the feeling doesn't go. He is still there, still inside the moment. Or it is in him. He is euphoric. He roars and his whole world shakes.

* *

"The first reaction is not fear. To fear properly, parely, you have to know what is happening, or at least to have narrowed down from all the vast range of possible happenings three or four that are appropriate to your circumstances; so not fear first, but something at once both less and more than fear, a true confusion – all systems down – the senses utterly overthrown."

Sam says.

The shock of being kidnapped renders your will immobile. You become a sitting target, an accomplice to your own abduction. The kidnapper recognises this and acts on it. The critical moment is the first moment. The difference between doing and being done to is, at its simplest, one of foreknowledge. The kidnapper always knows what is going to happen next, that is the advantage he has over you.

Ilse Klein, seeing Sam at the door of the Singer canteen this evening, turned around and tried to run back the way she had come. The wrong way, the way, she only later realised, he might have predicted she would run. He followed at her heels, pushing her between the shoulder-blades, causing her to stumble against a chair which she somehow, ridiculously, wound up sitting in, straight-backed, elbows behind her on a canteen table.

Clicking his fingers for the keys which she was still holding in her hand, Sam crossed the room and unlocked the chest refrigerator beneath the clock on the far wall and pulled from it three litre bottles of water.

"Here," he said.

He thrust the bottles into Ilse's arms and dragged her to her feet. She clutched the cold plastic to her chest, feeling the weight turn turbulent as she was bundled out into the night. Thirty seconds had elapsed since she had given in to his knocking and opened the door; in less than sixty he had her ramming a metal dumpster against a fencepost at the back of the canteen. The first two shoves shook the post, the third shove cracked it, the fourth lifted it clean out of the ground. Sam held the wire for her to crawl under and followed in behind her. Before them lay a border of waterlogged grass and beyond that the rain-slicked hump of the berm.

"Run," he said, and she did, without thinking, up and over.

They came down the far side a little way above the Frontierland Depot, well out of sight of the guard at the

Rivers of the Far West. At this time of night, Thunder Mesa was a ghost town. The spindly windmill creaked, polythene flapped in the windows of the ramshackle ranch; something tumbled, unseen, about the critterless Critter Corral. They had almost covered the open ground to the Trading Post when Sam laid hold of Ilse suddenly and trailed her into the deeper shadow of a doorway. Moments later a group of straggling workers passed, black and white hands shouldering spades, faces obscured by the hoods of their equalising yellow rain capes. Afterwards Sam realised he had forgotten to cover Ilse's mouth, but it was all right, for Ilse had forgotten she could scream. By the time she remembered he had collected himself and was holding the gun under her chin. She clasped the bottles tighter and together they walked the last few yards to Big Thunder Mountain. Halfway across she dropped a bottle into the soft mud and it sank instantly and without trace.

*

There was one moment early on in the mountain when Sam, having almost let his control slip that once, had to do something he didn't like so that there would be no doubting his deadly serious intent. Ilse Klein, binding Raymond Black's wrists, as Sam had instructed her (and a little recovered perhaps from her own first shock), had leaned her mouth in close to the Irishman's ear, even though they had been expressly forbidden to speak, and Sam had hit her, hard, with his half-closed fist on the side of her head. Her eyes flickered – she seemed for an instant genuinely surprised – then went dull.

After binding Ilse's hands too, Sam led her and Raymond up into the cathedral vastness of the mountain. They stopped when he told them to and waited in abject silence for his word to go again. At one point their ascent took them outside the mountain and Sam saw the long shadows of men still working by the light of arc lamps across the quagmire at the *Bazar* and someone was singing somewhere and the rain danced and darted in squalls above the roofs and towers and minarets, and it was beautiful in its chill night-time-in-the-city way.

Inside again, he marched Ilse and Raymond along the maintenance walkway moulded into the wall beside the rail track, until they arrived at a ledge commanding a view over a deep cavern from whose ceiling stalactites hung down among the scaffolding and the painters' platforms. On one side of the ledge, the track carried on into subterranean blackness, to surface again across the river-bed at the head of the Big Thunder Mining Company, and on the other side, back the way they had just come, the steel lines peaked in a dark blue arc of November night-sky. There was a door let into the mountain wall almost directly opposite the ledge, and facing that, a little below them, another, smaller passage opened at a favourable angle on to the track-side. It was an almost unassailably safe spot. Sam ordered Ilse and Raymond to sit with their backs turned to each other, but not touching, then he stepped down on to the track and placed the backpack where it could be seen from the ledge, pulling from it certain wires. He was still about this when a man appeared, swinging a flashlight, from the direction of the Mining Company. Beige cap, beige uniform, black boots: security guard. He was finishing a conversation with someone on his walkie-talkie, shaking his head and smiling to himself, when he caught sight of Sam standing in the middle of the track, aiming the gun, glaring out from behind his dreadful mudman mask.

In fact, Sam was having to struggle to keep himself from cracking it laughing. This whole thing was going so smoothly – the timing of each escalation was so effortlessly perfect – that he might almost, without realising, have tapped into some inverse Disney synchronicity: a sequence of events destined to be repeated at this time every day until just such an intervention as his set in train the park's undoing; as though each thing was bound by nature to contain within it the code of its own negation.

All animation had faded from the security guard's features. He stood, stalled, walkie-talkie arrested midway between hip and chin. Sam regarded him a moment or two longer, trying to fit him into the pattern.

"You understand English?" he asked and the guard nodded unhappily. "OK, listen to me. Lay the radio on the ground – that's right – now walk back down there and when you get outside tell them I have something very important I want to say. Tell them I have dy-na-mite."

The guard backed down the track, disappearing in irregular, bobbing stages, like a series of ever more anxious curtsies; black boots, beige uniform, beige cap. When nothing of him remained to be seen his voice rose up in a wail to fill the absence.

"A la bombe! A la bombe! Terroriste!"

Gary arrived about two hours later. He is some kind of diplomat, from the embassy in Paris. Sam pictures him in full evening dress; imagines the urgent message delivered to his box at the Opéra; the whispered apologies; the blue flashing lights of the motorcade. Or perhaps that is not the sort of diplomat he is at all. Perhaps Gary sits alone in a starkly-lit, limited-access room, smoking cigarettes, drinking bourbon from a bottle stored in the drawer of a filing cabinet retained expressly for that purpose, studying photographs through a magnifying glass, listening to tapes of freaky sex.

Gary was maybe the fifth person Sam had spoken to in those two hours. Inverse synchronicity. It all went on as you would expect it to go on, like clockwork. Each of the previous three voices had sounded a little less incredulous than the one before. Sam patiently repeated his single demand.

Yes, he said, they heard him right.

Gary's voice, when it came over the airwaves, was all unruffable professionalism. *Uh-huh, uh-huh, I see, I see,* though it was plain that he did not, for the first thing he did when Sam had finished speaking was ask him to release one of his hostages. As if Sam could. Gary carried on, unperturbed, asking Sam had he not heard the news from the Lebanon (Tom Sutherland and Terry Waite had been freed —tonight, of all nights, was no time for an American, of all people, to go taking hostages), explaining to Sam why it was he and not someone from the company who was going to be conducting negotiations from this point on. He sold himself like a service. *Guaranteed 100 per cent impartiality. . . Ears of people back in the US. . .*

Yeah, yeah, yeah.

It was all one to Sam. He didn't care who was out there talking, there was nothing to negotiate. He would tell his story as often as they would listen to it, he would tell it even when there was no one left to listen. But no negotiating, and no hostage releases. They don't seem to understand, three in the mountain is not simply one more than two.

Like a moth emerging from a chrysalis into a flytrap, Ilse Klein struggles from her stupor into the tight wrap of the blanket. Sam feels her move beside him, a series of twitches and spasms as she makes a mental inspection of her body, visiting each outpost in turn. When she has finished, her back against his left arm rises and falls in a silent sigh.

"Are you OK?" Sam asks.

She starts at his voice, but collects herself and makes a smothered laugh sound. Her neck is stiff, her wrists are raw, her feet are numb – she has a throbbing pain above one ear – and for the last several hours she has been under constant threat of death.

"I suppose I am all right," she says.

These are the first words she has spoken to him since she opened the door of the Singer canteen. Her voice is quiet but bitter. Sam regrets this. He regrets having had to hit her earlier. He tells her now he is sorry. Again she smothers a laugh.

"*Hey, I said I'm sorry.*"

His anger comes all at once, from nowhere.

"No," Ilse says, hurriedly, "it was not that I was laughing at, I was only thinking" – her head rotates within the restricted arc permitted by the blanket – "the shadow," she says: "look at the shadow."

Across the track at an angle from them. It is an image of a mountain projected on to the mountain wall; a mountain sculpted with their profiles; magnified, monumental. Ilse, having drawn his attention to it, senses instantly she has blundered because it is difficult to remain unimpressed by so dramatic an expansion, and Sam, she thinks, needs little encouragement. The image holds a moment longer, then the light swings round and the shadow leaps behind them before merging with the darkness pouring down the shaft towards the mine entrance. Ilse straightens her shoulders. Her hair moves, unleashing smells of English canteen dinners: pizza slices with tinned-corn topping, boiled turnip, and something they call savoury mince. She breathes twice, steadying her voice, and asks Sam to untie her hands. Sam is taken aback by her directness. Now it is he who laughs.

"I won't run away," she tells him.

"I'd shoot you if you tried," he tells her.

"Precisely, so I will not run away."

He considers this a half a second before saying no. She gives up. Too easily, Sam thinks.

"Don't worry," he says. "I know they're there."

"Who?"

"*Who!*"

His laughter this time is spiteful. Ilse makes no reply.

"You know who," he says. "The guys hiding down the track, I've seen them too."

"I'm sorry, I don't understand."

He throws his right arm out suddenly over her shoulder. Ilse can't help it, she jumps and makes a noise that she does not recognise as coming from her. The butt of the gun is only a few inches from her face. The barrel looks out parallel with her eyes.

46

"There," he says.

For a moment it passes through Ilse's mind to bite his wrist. She despises him for making her jump like that. She will bite, she thinks, and not let go. Right in the middle of the tendons. He cannot do anything to her with the gun while she has his wrist in her mouth. He will scream, release the blanket; the other hostage, the Irishman, Raymond, might be able to get up, to kick him. The police will come quickly. She believes she *did* see shapes just then, not far off, retreating as the light moved round.

But then there is the bag on the track to consider, the dynamite. They cannot come quickly enough to stop him exploding that.

He raises his arm off her shoulder and points round the vault at random.

"And there," he says, "and there, and there, and there."

He has brought the radio out by this time and begun shouting into it.

"They are all over the place and if they don't back off in thirty seconds, I swear to Christ, these people in here are dead."

There is a pause followed by indistinct sounds of movement. Gary's voice appears in the chamber, mollifying.

"It's not what you think, Sam. We only wanted to see everyone in there was still all right."

"Never better," Sam says.

Ilse hears him scratch at his face and hears the pitter of dried mud flaking off on to his collar. That is how close their heads are. She hears too the mashing of his tongue in his mouth. Whenever he is not speaking out loud he hums and mutters little bits of this and that under his breath. It is as though a spring has broken, a stop mechanism. She recognises these symptoms, this is what she tried to whisper to the Irishman, Raymond, when she was tying his hands: to be careful, not to do anything rash, that this Sam was unpredictable. And then, of course – *smack!* – at that very moment (her ear, thought about, throbs) he proved her right by hitting out at her. But Raymond in any case was completely cowed. She realises how foolish she was just now to think she could count on him for help.

She moves her fingers behind her back, trying to keep the circulation going, trying not to touch the American. She wishes suddenly that Konrad was here. Konrad the Resourceful, with his quick hands and his penknife; Konrad the Brave, making bullets out of pebbles wrapped in foil, sleeping with his six gun under his pillow to guard the house against the Indians, and the Russians if they came. Konrad would have known what to do in a situation like this.

But sentimental thoughts will only drag her down again and she cannot allow herself to sink back into her former pupate state. She must have hope, but she must also be reasonable. So, Konrad is a grown man, with a grown man's thick fingers, and in all probability does not even know, much less care, where his sister is. Unless the authorities are trying even now to trace him. She *must* phone him, first thing, when she gets out of here and tell him that she is safe. She will have a bath and a proper sleep and the next day she will go and visit him. Pepe will just have to manage somehow.

Yes.

She feels cheered by the prospect of seeing her brother again. They cannot stay angry with each other for ever. She uses her chin to pull the blanket a little further up her neck where there is a draught. The blanket moves and instantly the draught drops three feet to the gap between her work socks and her trousers. She almost laughs.

Raymond the Irishman snorts and moans. (Sam the American carries on muttering over the top of it.) He snorts again and yawns. They are sounds such as a man might make waking up in a train carriage, say, full of strangers – self-conscious, but not embarrassed, because after all everyone falls asleep on the train at some time or other. But soon it comes back to him exactly where he is, that this is no train carriage. His body stiffens then sags. Ilse feels each stage of his awakening on her side of the blanket. She wants to offer him some encouragement, to tell him not to be afraid and not, whatever he does, to let himself go again. She is, though, a little bit afraid herself. She recalls earlier the sickening blow to her head and she does not want to provoke a second. There must be another way. She ponders for a time then remembers the Irish bars in Berlin and the songs she used to hear sung there. There is one, she thinks, in which a boy is hanged . . . on a gallows tree? A sad song, but beautiful. How does it go? She begins absentmindedly to whistle it, at first letting fall only crumbs of the tune, then accenting maybe one note in every two, two notes in every three. Even with this little she believes there is some response. She becomes bolder, more fluent, as the song comes back to her, until finally, just as she is beginning to forget herself altogether, Sam tugs the blanket and cuts her short.

"Quiet," he says.

Ilse complies at once, but her purpose has been achieved. The breathing coming from the opposite end has quickened. There is, at last, life about it.

*

He cannot quite believe it to begin with, but in the end Raymond has to conclude that the German woman from the Singer canteen is indeed whistling "Kevin Barry". His pulse quickens as he braces himself for whatever it is this new and precise taunt heralds. He cannot turn his head to look at her, of course, so he does not know whether she is doing this under duress, whether the American is, quite literally, holding a gun to her head. Perhaps, next, Raymond will be forced to serenade her with the theme from *The Dambusters*. But it is the American himself who shuts her up (Raymond's head jerks with the blanket, a more violent approval than he actually feels) and he abandons all hope of understanding. Everything has gone haywire today. Or perhaps there is nothing unusual about today at all, perhaps the past eight years have merely been a hiatus and today has set him back on the abnormal course he plotted for himself the night he agreed to get into a car in Belfast with Gillespie and Ollie Thompson. There is, undeniably, a sense of an action being concluded in all this, a certain perverse symmetry in a door being opened and a man in a mask of mud standing on the threshold pointing a gun at his head.

Sam has more to thank doors for than he yet knows.

*

When May asked Raymond, centuries ago it seems like tonight, at the end of his first day home, what the hardest thing was to get used to he said, without thinking, the doors. He should have said, of course, seeing all the family in the one room at the one time, or being in bed with her again after so many years. He *might*, just as easily, have said the width of the sky or the length of the streets, but the doors were what were in his mind at the precise moment she asked him and the doors were what he said he found hardest to get used to. Doors you could enter and leave as you pleased any time of the night or day.

May, misinterpreting him, started in then crying again.

"You can't blame people wanting a bit of a change," she said.

(The front doors on the street where they lived – the street where Raymond grew up – used to be pale blue. All the doors, always. The doors were pale blue and the window frames were white. They were painted every five years and it was a great feeling when the painters had gone and the street gleamed like brand new. But when the car turned into the street that first morning back he had seen yellow doors and red doors and mahogany doors, doors with brass knockers and carriage lamps and stained-glass insets; and tucked away in among them, like a last standard of the familiar, a solitary pale blue one, his and May's. May said it was the first thing people did when they bought over their houses, changed the doors. *What for?* he asked her. *Do they think they're on* **Dallas**?)

"You don't understand," he said.

"No," May said, "you don't."

She bit her lip to keep it from trembling and reached for her cigarettes. Berkeleys. Long and inelegant. She smoked, not looking at him. She had had silver streaks put in her hair for him coming home and there were red bows on the shoulders of her new black nightie. She chewed a ragnail and spat the skin off her lip on to the duvet. Stephanie's card stood, splayed, on the chest of drawers at his side of the bed. *Weclome Home Daddy* the message read.

"It's spelt wrong," she had told him, disappointed.

"This isn't going to work," May said.

The Berkeley sizzled, a black stone at the heart of its orange glow.

Next day she told him there was someone else.

"Who?" he asked.

"Does it matter?" she said.

In fact, she was right, it didn't matter at all. She said the name anyway. It held no unpleasant memories for him. A perfectly good man.

"He was going to come and talk to you," May said, "but

I wouldn't let him. I wanted to give us a chance first."

"I'm glad you did," he said.

He felt on one level an immense relief. May was studying his face, trying to read behind it.

"You're not going to go and do anything, now, are you?" she said.

She was smoking another of her big Berkeleys. She held it as though balancing the ash was the whole point.

"Of course I'm not," he said.

When she had left the room he sat in the armchair, trying to think. May had made a shelf for her books beside the TV; a box top backed with wallpaper and then painted. The spines of the books were all pastels, or black with ornate silver and gold lettering. There was a Bible there too and the narrow rainbow stripes of the child's Ladybirds. It was the exactness of the fit that convinced him there was no room for him there, not in May's house, not in his parents' house, not anywhere in that area. There was, though, no question of him leaving Belfast, at least not then. Despite everything, Belfast was still his city. It was instinctive in him, a city of shortcuts and sudden turns learnt as a child holding unthinking to his mother's hand, of bus routes and fare stages got by heart, and the inevitability of relatives' houses. It was a story for every landmark and pothole, a spontaneous remembrance of a brown-coloured photograph each time he passed the spot where his great-grandfather had fallen from his bicycle under the wheels of the Donegall Road tram. On the day that his eyes were first opened to the world beyond his parents' faces, Belfast was offered to him complete; it brimmed but somehow made room for him; he swam in it and felt it flood him.

He switched on the television, looking for Channel 4, but all he got was fuzz. He was on his knees, fiddling with the tuner, when Stephanie entered.

"Channel 4's wrecked," she said.

She stayed over by the door, one hand on the handle.

"Is it?" he said and she said *Uh-huh*.

May came back in.

"Your daddy's going away again, Stephie," she said, looking at him.

Stephanie nodded.

"Back to prison?" she asked.

Indirectly.

*

From Belfast to Glasgow by Larne-Stranraer, through Edinburgh to Aberdeen then Sunderland via Gateshead. Shopping centres and superstores. Stockton Darlington Bradford Leeds. In Liverpool it was Albert Dock, in Wigan it was the Pier. Warrington was the centre of Britain. Software Parks and Enterprise Zones, even, sometimes, houses. Nottingham Norwich Birmingham Cardiff – London for a time then north again to Manchester. He built home out of his system and into everyone else's. A brick here, a brick there. He hooked up with a crew heading down to the Chunnel and, when the jobs began drying up there, took a boat with them in the direction they had been digging, only to become separated from them somewhere in northern France, which was how it came about that almost seven years after he left Belfast he found himself standing alone one morning before the wonderful world of Euro Disney.

Sitting now with his hands tied in Big Thunder Mountain, it feels like a long way round to right back where he started from.

*

"Hey, Raymond. You with us again? You want some water?"

The tight halter of the blanket is relaxed a little allowing Raymond to turn his chin in line with his shoulder. He sees the blue plastic bottle, the gun, and the face in between them in that order. Mud is peeling here and there from the face. The skin underneath is stained the colour of barley sugar. The mouth is formed into a smile, as if this was some kind of party game they were playing.

The blue plastic *O* is pressed to Raymond's lips, he tilts his chin and the bottle rises with it. He doesn't know how long it is since he last had anything to drink. His throat resists, but he gulps the water down none the less, using his tongue to stem the flow now and then while he swallows through the pain.

"Had enough?"

"Mm."

Raymond sucks another mouthful as the bottle begins to draw away. The last few drops trickle across his cheek and round behind his ear. He brings his shoulder up to cut them off before they get inside his clothes and as he does so he catches sight of the German woman's head. (*Ilse*: her name is Ilse.) Only the back of it is visible and for the few seconds he is turned looking at her it remains completely motionless, yet in spite of this he experiences the peculiar sensation that something is being communicated to him. Facing away again, he is confronted by the stalactites he and Nat Stanley were painting today. He remembers the thousands of labour hours that have gone into making them and the walls that surround him and for the first time it occurs to him that the people out there are not going to let this guy blow up the mountain.

His relief, though, is short-lived. *Let* suggests that they are in control, or even that Sam is; as if explosives were docile substances, like plasticine, or tripe. This is not Raymond's experience of them. A week or two before his parole he had spent some time in the prison hospital with a man who had carried out three car bombings back in the Seventies. The man, *X*, had developed stomach cancer after only nine years of the three hundred-odd he had been sentenced to. It was heads they won, tails he lost, he said: if the cancer was operable he was in here for life, if the authorities released him he was going to die. The judge at his trial had called the car bomb a heinous and despicable device. X disagreed. The car bomb, he said, was one of the major military innovations of the twentieth century. (Along with joyriding and De Lorean, he told Raymond, it was also one of Northern Ireland's few contributions to its defining cultural obsession, the automobile.) The car bomb was pure function: the medium was the message. (The prisons of Northern Ireland were full of philosophers and semioticians.) Even saying the words. Carbomb! It was, what do you call it, *onomatopoeia*.

You fought with what was to hand. If you had factories, the resources of the capitalist state to call on, you made beautifully compact anti-personnel grenades, elegant surface-to-surface missiles. If all you had was what you could rustle up on the street, you made tin-can grenades and car bombs.

At the time of his arrest X was in his mid-forties. He was about to become a grandfather for the first time, was well respected locally for his work with boys' clubs.

"There were three of us assembling these things in a mate's garage," he said, the way you might say there were three of us reconditioning the engine. "It was hairy enough sometimes."

One of his bombs had been filmed going off and had become a classic of its type. It was still shown in documentaries with names like *The Troubles in Ireland*, or *Ulster: The Unending Pain*. He had had a letter from a friend in New Zealand who had seen it down there, and another letter, circuitously (and, finally, anally), from a Maoist theatre collective who had used it, slowmo'd, as the centre of a multi-media performance at the Edinburgh Fringe. If he had been paid royalties every time that bit of film was shown, he said, he would be a wealthy man by now.

Raymond remembered having seen the film too. Its televisual appeal was obvious. The car – it was an Austin Maxi, *lovely car, the Maxi*, X said – sat for a second, viewed from behind an army pig, looking pristine and intact, innocent even: wrongly accused. (At that very moment, X explained to Raymond, the detonation had already begun. Molecules were metamorphosing, what was inert had now become charged.) Then its integrity suddenly went and it was hard watching the film to separate the car from the explosives, to remember that this was not the result of some intrinsic flaw, a thing that cars just *did*, hyper-combusting, and at the same time as you were thinking this you heard the bang and the loss of form became specifically smoke and shrapnel, and a soldier in the foreground ducked and there was the sound, verging on overdub, of glass shattering.

The beauty of the Maxi, X said, was the boot. If ever there was a car built to be a bomb it was the Maxi. Raymond thought of the three men working in their garage. That they had made this. There was a certain ingenuity in it. Perhaps there was, too, a value in keeping it on film. Perhaps, as X said, that fifteen-second clip, properly considered, said more about what was happening then than the hours of flaccid commentary that surrounded it. Why would three men, all with families, none with police records, want to spend their evenings in a garage making bombs? (For the same reason, of course, that three friends, one just married, with their entire adult lives before them would steal a car and go looking around for someone to kill.)

There were no clips of the other two bombs, because there

was no time for the cameras to arrive before they went off. No time even to clear the streets. It was the stupid fella at the *Irish News* one time, X said, wrote down Y street when what they had said was Z; and the other time it was a new fertiliser mix they were using, and to cap it all they couldn't find a flaming phone-box working.

Seven people died in the two explosions, scores more were injured.

X smoked an illicit cigarette.

"Of course," he said, "if we'd had the stuff they have to work with today none of that would ever have happened."

But Raymond by that stage had already begun to drift away.

He is adrift again here, now, tonight in the mountain. In some part of his brain he understands that he should try and stop himself and yet it is so much less painful this way, to become detached from what is being inflicted on you, to be as unresisting as a baby, dropped. He hears a voice, Sam's voice, unravelling like a bucket descending a well. Soon he will not hear it any more. He will not hear the blast if it comes, or the bullet; he will not feel them.

Ilse senses him slipping back and senses in herself a small bereavement. She will not, though, despair. Ilse is not ignorant of the nature of bombs herself, but even so she does not think that those outside will let this one explode, and actually she chooses to believe that Sam is right on one score, that anyone who can conjure all this, a virtual city, out of beet fields and marshland, in months, not years, can surely come up with another mouse by morning.

There! Spoken like a true little *Besatzungskind*.

Her mother would turn in her grave to hear her describe herself so, but it is true, she thinks – has always thought: all the children she grew up with, not just the ones with milk chocolate skin, or those whose mothers waited every month for money orders from Seattle or Minneapolis, but *all* of them, in a sense, were sons and daughters of the Occupying Forces.

When Ilse was a child she went with her father and her brother Konrad to Uncle Erich's American Cinema. Stuttgart then was still a city of gaps and holes. Views opened up suddenly across vast bowls of weeds and grasses and broken brick to the bristling hills; streets came to ragged halts, like the sentences of the adults when Ilse and Konrad entered a room, disappearing into the black dots of the unspoken.

The cinema stood at the corner of a levelled square close to the cathedral; a bare cinder-block box surrounded by dust and slung with coloured bulbs. Inside, to the right of the kiosk where Uncle Erich sat all day smoking his Lucky Strike cigarettes, was a little shrine made up of covers from the magazines he swapped with the Amis: Joan Crawford, Carole Lombard, Ava Gardner, Wendy Barrie, Gloria Grahame, Jane Russell, Lauren Bacall, and, at its centre, Uncle Erich's own favourite screen goddess, Jean Harlow. Ilse would try to recite the names while her father struck a match, one-handed, and smoked a cigarette with Uncle Erich. There was a hole too at the end of her father's sleeve where his other hand should have come down, though sometimes the hole was filled by a brown leather sheath with a claw on the end. Ilse's father had lost the hand long long ago on the Russian Front. Ilse's prayer when she was a child was that someone would find the hand – frozen in the ice, perhaps, exactly where he dropped it – and send it home. Her mother's prayer then, repeated every night after the *Vaterunser*, kneeling with Ilse at the foot of her bed, was for all the wives and mothers who looked at a space at their dinner table and wept. There was no space at her own table because God had given her Ilse to sit in Maria's seat. Maria was three when she was carried off by Asiatic flu. Whenever Ilse thought about her sister she heard the beating of wings and saw Maria slung sleeping in a hammock borne by four black-haired angels. Once when she had the flu herself she felt her fevered body lift off and hover for a time above the sickbed until a hand on her forehead brought her back to the sound of her mother singing:

> Bo bee Shaf toze gone to *sea*,
> Sil ver bu kelz on his *knee*,
> He ll come back and ma ree *me*,
> Bo nee Bo bee
> Shaf
> toe.

Ilse's mother sang to her in three languages. Her name was Isabelle and she came from wayfaraway in Strasbourg. She had left there (*crossed the Rhine*, was how she said it) as a young woman to study German at the university in Freiburg, where her own mother was born. In the evenings she gave French and English lessons to a melancholy young clerk by the name of Günter who worked for his uncle, a merchant, in the Snail Quarter. Sometimes after lessons he would walk her back to her pension on the Herrenstrasse, his voice so airy with dreams it was scarcely audible above the lapping of the *Bächle* flowing through the streets of the Old Town. When he first proposed to her, Isabelle said no and went back to Strasbourg to try to forget him. But he would not let her forget and came for her the next summer, and the next summer, and asked again and again until finally she gave him the answer he sought. This time when she crossed the Rhine she did not go to Freiburg, but to Stuttgart, where Günter's parents lived. For a year or two they were wonderfully happy, as a young man and woman ought to be, just married.

Then the war came and Ilse's father lost his hand on the Russian Front and Maria came and the French came and then the war was over and the Americans came and Konrad came and Maria was carried away by the black-haired angels and Ilse came and then it was now and Ilse's father took her to Uncle Erich's cinema by the cathedral.

Before the war her father had worked in the town hall and even after he returned from Russia without his hand they took him in again and gave him back his old desk. When the Americans came, however, he was made to leave his job and then he had to take his chance with the rest and find what work he could. Often this meant no work at all. When he arrived at the cinema some days he would pat his pockets, frowning at his forgetfulness until Uncle Erich said, No, Günter, and offered him his box of Luckies. Of course, Uncle Erich let them all into the cinema free of charge, on good days as well as bad, and often after the film had finished he gave the children each a tin from the back of his kiosk to take home. American tins, Campbell's and Chef Boyardee, condensed soup and meatballs.

In their stomachs and their heads, then, even if not in their genes, *Besatzungskinder*.

Ilse could not have been more than four or five by the time the worst was over. Her father was reinstated, once and for all, in the town hall and took her to the movies less and less. More and more new buildings appeared, stopping the gaps in the Stuttgart streets. Uncle Erich's cinder-block cinema was bulldozed eventually when the square by the cathedral was restored. He left the city shortly afterwards, turning up again at intervals throughout Ilse's childhood. Gradually, however, as Ilse's parents changed houses, restoring their own lives, they lost contact altogether. Then one day, years later (Ilse's parents had not long moved into a small villa in the Höhenlage), an aerogramme arrived from Cairo, where it seemed Uncle Erich was now living. He had gone out there some months before, with no intention of staying, he said, until an Egyptian friend had taken him to the Great Pyramid (yes, Uncle Erich climbing) and he had seen in the distance the City of the Dead, a veritable township of mausoleums, where lesser dignitaries than the pharaohs had their resting places. Dust rose from the regular ochre streets, mingling with smoke from fires – *cooking* fires, his companion insisted. The City of the Dead was alive with people – thousands upon thousands of them, Uncle Erich later learnt: squatters, eating, sleeping, making love among the sarcophagi. Shops and schools had begun to spring up, power and water were being requested. In time, no doubt, the living population would outgrow the tombs; more houses would have to be built and the City of the Dead would itself be buried under new developments, just as the graves of those who had built the tombs, and the pyramids before them, had long ago been erased.

Actually, Uncle Erich wrote, looking down from the slope of the pyramid it reminded him a lot of Stuttgart after the war. He had drawn them a cramped diagram, showing an intersection of streets, arrows pointing this way and that – the city, the desert, the Red Sea – and in the middle a circled dot and above it a caricature of his own smiling face.

"Every city needs its cinema," he wrote.

Sam Raymond and Ilse sitting in huff formation, tightly bound: gabbler drifter grim believer. Three ways of looking at the inside of a mountain. Three histories flaring at random, like their three faces coming and going in the wheeling unavoidable lights.

"Sam?"

Gary. Something in the voice, even Raymond stirs.

"Sam, good news.

"Sam?

"They've questioned the foreman, from the other week, you remember? They've checked out your story. He's confessed – you were right – it was misconduct, no doubt about it. The contractors have been told, either they discipline him or they're off the job. Isn't that great news?

"And, Sam, tomorrow morning they're going to start going through their records till they find the name of the other guy, the, ah, one who fell in the mud. See, didn't I tell you? We can soon have this whole thing sorted out. What do you say?"

Ilse and Raymond listen expectantly, as well they might. After the non-stop commentary of the past six hours, however, the silence that suddenly yawns between them is so absolute it seems to suck into it all the myriad noises of the surrounding night. Bat sonar and train brakes, the breathing of bomb-disposal men.

"Sam?"

"I'm sorry," he says, and, to do him justice, sounds it. "It's not enough any more."

He switches off the radio. The uncanny silence returns, deepens, if that is possible, and then unaccountably, and very quietly, he begins to cry.

Ilse and Raymond are horrified. A man in tears is one thing, a man in tears in control of a gun and a bomb – with your life in his hands – is quite another. For two, maybe three, minutes there is no let-up. His crying chills them, like a child's inexplicable night-time mewling. Ilse has to restrain herself from reaching back with her fingers at one stage to comfort him, Raymond for a moment is on the point of humming a lullaby. A lullaby. *This man is their kidnapper. This man would have them dead.*

He sobs a full minute longer then his body changes gear and begins to tremble violently. Ilse and Raymond do all they can to stop themselves but nevertheless tremble with him. The gun waggles between them, a gimcrack metronome, and clunks once against Raymond's hard hat. (He had forgotten till that moment he was even wearing it.) He gasps. It feels as if the blanket will no longer be able to hold them and for some reason that has become something to be feared. The trembling worsens. Now the walls of the mountain themselves seem to vibrate, as though they too were about to break apart.

Oh fuck.

Raymond turns his head a split second after Ilse, straining his neck, trying to get a fix on the bag down there on the rail track, thinking – what exactly? that he will be able to *outface* the bomb, or that actually seeing it go off will somehow protect him? His mouth falls open, his brain broils with oaths of outrage, but it is Sam's voice that speaks into the void:

"What's your favourite colour?"

The trembling peaks, but is contained. Ilse and Raymond are dumbstruck.

"What's your favourite colour? What's your favourite colour?"

"Purple," they blurt in unison.

One final shudder, then the trembling stops altogether.

"Hey, mine too," Sam says and he starts to giggle.

*

Sam is not stupid. At certain moments he understands perfectly well why these things are happening to him. He has been wired for ten days solid, it is no surprise if now and then his body is not his own. It is all a part of the speed deal and he does not feel as if he has lost out on it.

That last stuff he scored, though, at the beginning of the weekend, was something else again. The pusher (is the wrong word, Sam was an open door) in the Buttes-Chaumont park had promised him he would not have had anything like it before. Just arrived, he said, from Łódź. Sam had never heard of the place. In Poland, the pusher told him.

He was counting off Sam's change, switching a match from one side of his mouth to the other. Sam thought bizarrely of the lobster fishermen he sometimes saw, as a boy in Maine, striking their deals over tanks of shifting shells. Money seemed such an unimaginative medium for what they, and the pusher, had to exchange. The Polish factories were working flat out these days to keep Paris fuelled, the man said, calling after Sam as he hurried towards the park gate: *Un ban pour l'entreprise privée. Hein?* Three cheers for private enterprise!

The way this particular stuff is – you take as much of it as Sam has taken at any rate – it seems to be leading you one place, then halfway through the trip you find you're headed somewhere else altogether. There are snakes waiting at the top of its golden ladders, and escalators, jauntily lit, rising suddenly out of its darkest pits. Sam is pretty well adjusted to these switches by now, as untroubled by them as he would be by sneezing if he had a cold. Like sneezing, everything just turns inward for a second or two, helplessly focused on that chain reaction, and then – *blam!* – a shake of the head and it's carry on as before. What he has no knowledge of as yet is the crash. It must be nine hours since his last hit, just before he set out from the park in Esbly. He remembers folding the stuff away carefully in his coat pocket but when he felt for it again a little later – as he was leading Ilse and Raymond up here from the storeroom – the pocket was empty. All he can think is that it fell out when he stripped off in front of the mud pool. But, this is the weird thing, he is not panicking. His mind is still focused and he knows that if he can hold out till seven he will be all right.

Forget the frigging foreman. Once Mort gets here, *everything* will be straight.

*

"Have you any idea how unlikely that is?" Sam asks them. "All three of us?"

He is pretty certain the more he thinks about it that purple is his favourite colour.

"I mean, first you would have to count all the colours there were in the world, that's all the colours *and* all the shades of all the colours, then raise that to the power of three. That's the likelihood. Do you hear that, Raymond? Ilse? That's the *un*likelihood."

Sam has this vision – more real than an idea, real enough almost that he could take a picture of it – of a quotient with a spastic colon, pumping zeroes, filling the chamber, like spawn.

There are moments tonight (this is one) when he looks back and his whole life seems to have been a winding-in of a piece of string leading him to here.

But Raymond and Ilse are still too shaken, or too angry, to respond, so rather than have the night go flat Sam takes up the conversation again.

"When I was in elementary school there was this kid in my class, Calvin Lee his name was, who was – oh, Jesus, a really great kid and everything, but a math *nut*. Like his brother – Tony? – we were, uh, let's see – yeah, nine – Tony died of, I forget, something in the brain, a tumour I guess it must have been, and every time anyone went near Calvin to tell him how sorry they were he just shrugged and told them what the chances were of them dying too by the time they were twelve. He had worked it out: so many thousand to one. Can you believe that?"

(Can you believe this? When Sam was in elementary school he was embarrassed sometimes to say his own name and, sometimes, found it easier when meeting people he didn't know to make his mouth call him . . .)

"And another thing about

(. . . Calvin Lee.)

"Calvin Lee. . .

(*Can I be you and you be me?*)

"His mom and dad had promised to take him to Disney World for his tenth birthday, the year after Tony died. They told him he could bring a school-friend along on the trip. Calvin strung it out for weeks before making his mind up. We all had a one in thirty-two chance, he kept saying, right to the end, though some kids, of course, the kids who had known him the longest or played with him the most, thought they had a better chance than the others. But maybe he really did do it the scientific way, maybe he did put all the names into a big bag and draw one out blind, because he chose me, who he hardly knew and almost never talked to. I ran all the way home from school – this was, uh, we had just moved into a house – an apartment, actually, over a store right in the middle of town. Holly and Tom, that's my own mom and dad, were in their workshop out back, varnishing pots. They came round from behind their workbenches when I told them, wiping their hands, real slow, like they were trying to take it in. Tom crouched down in front of me and took me by the wrist. Do *you* want to go, Sam? he said.

"I was nine years old.

"He started in to some big explanation about how they had bought up the land down there in Orlando and then repeated his question: Do you *really* want to go? I just looked at the rafters. I was thinking about the pirates Calvin had told me they had in Disney World, robots that walked and talked like real human beings.

"It's not like the cartoons you see on TV, you know, Holly said. It's all commercialised. Do you understand what that is? It's all false. Tom glanced over his shoulder at her, like *what do we do now?* It was a kind of rule they had that as long as we talked everything through together they would never say no to anything I asked for. But this was the first time I'd asked for something they wouldn't have wanted for me anyway. They spent the evening making calls to their old hippy pals out in the boondocks. There was a whole bunch of them had lived together in this kind of commune way back in the Sixties when they first arrived from LA.

"Oh, *man*, I heard one of them say when Tom told him what I wanted to do.

"The vote was split five to four in favour of letting me go. When I got back from Orlando, though, they were all there —I mean, they tried to make it look like a party, you know: first time away from home; but what it was, I think, they were waiting to debrief me. It was weird, there were all these neat-looking cars parked out front, new models a few of them, and inside it was like Woodstock revisited. People sitting on the floor, little kiddies running around barefoot. There was a smell out in the kitchen, I wasn't dumb, even then I knew somebody had been smoking grass.

"And the expressions on their faces, when I came in the door . . . ? I can't describe them. I felt, I don't know, like the dove sent out from the Ark, like they were hoping I would come back and tell them everything was OK, they had won through.

"So, Tom said, how was *Dizzy* World?

"Everyone had on these real tight smiles.

"All it is is a bunch of dumb rides, I said, and you could see straight off, the way their mouths relaxed, what a big relief it was. Later, when I went to my room, I could hear them kidding around. Somebody was taking off the Goof's voice only the joke was it was supposed to be President Carter giving a speech about the price of gas or whatever it was they were always talking about in those days. They were laughing like crazy.

"Calvin's mom and dad had bought me a Mickey Mouse

watch. I hadn't meant not to mention it, just when I came in and saw everyone looking at me like that. . . I took it to my room and lay listening to the laughing from the lounge, following Mickey's finger as he pointed out the minutes, like he'd made them all up or something off the top of his head. It was the first secret I'd ever had from Holly and Tom. I hid the watch in a plastic bag out the back of the stable they used as a workshop and only wore it when I went to school. Even after the dew got into the bag and the watch stopped I wore it, and when the strap broke I kept it with me, in my pocket, as a kind of talisman. Every day, without fail. I still had it when I arrived in France. I still had it right up until a couple of weeks ago. But when I finally made it back to Paris from here I took it out of my pocket as I was crossing over the river and dropped it off the bridge into the water."

*

Let's get one thing straight, when Sam arrived into work that Monday morning, the morning before the afternoon on the Pont Marie, there was no hint, visible or spoken, of the heresy that would turn him, two weeks later, into the hostage-taker you see now holed up in Big Thunder Mountain. On the contrary, at twenty-two, he was, in manner and outlook, even in appearance, a model of Disney orthodoxy. While a senior in college in southern Texas, he had written a paper (subsequently published, to local acclaim, as *The Railroad and the Storyboard: Journeys to the Heart of the American Psyche*) in which he had argued a symbolic link between the railroads of the nineteenth century and the motion picture industry in the opening years of our own. One the ultimate expression of a physically expanding frontier, the other – growing up at the westward limits of the continent – its final abstraction into the endlessly elastic realms of the imagination. Nowhere were the new frontiers pushed further than in the animated film, "the art of the seeming impossible", in Sam's own words, and no one flouted those impossibilities better than Walter Elias Disney – himself (Sam had been building to this point for three and a half pages) an avowed railroad enthusiast. Indeed these two elements, motion pictures and trains, the twin passions of Disney's early life, were brought together in the idea that came to dominate the closing years of it, the eponymous theme parks – magic kingdoms, pleasure cities, call them what you will – that stood as his lasting physical monuments. They were films you could inhabit, ringed around with a railroad, laced with lesser tracks, like subplots, with a wienie, as Walt liked to say, at the end of every street, to keep the whole thing moving.

Sam had visited Disney World a second time in his sophomore year with Bethan, another Mainer – *Maniac*, she would keep saying – whom he was notionally dating at the time: fey ironists whose interest it soon transpired extended no further than It's a Small World. Sam split from them after an hour and spent the rest of the trip exploring on his own. He didn't date Bethan again. He spent weekends in other parks – Disney Wannabes all, and all lacking the vital Disney coherence. In one, he took a ride on the copycat perimeter railroad, but a little way out of the first station, something jammed up front and the engine came to a complete stop. To begin with the passengers sat patiently in the midday sun, perhaps thinking this was all part of the entertainment, while the train's cast members tried to sort out the "problem". After a minute or two, however, a tape loop started up announcing their arrival in another part of the park and people began looking at their neighbours, a little sheepish, but smiling. By the time the tape had gotten around to hoping everyone had enjoyed the ride and telling them to come again soon, with the train still stuck where it had stopped ten minutes before, they were hanging over the sides of the cars, laughing; kids were stomping their feet or jumping up and down on their seats. The cast members had passed far beyond embarrassment. Sam caught the eye of one guy, a Vietnamese, twenty, twenty-one, and he saw real fear in it. Cars were shaking now; if the engine hadn't finally started when it did, Sam thought it was entirely possible that the guests in their hilarity would have taken it to pieces. Taken it to pieces, perhaps, and rampaged on out through the park.

"Continuity of motion", his paper went on, "is to the theme park what persistency of vision is to the animated film: a *sine qua non*. If movement is impeded for too long, or too often, the illusion falters, as surely as if the film stutters in the projector or freezes mid-frame. The longer the break in the flow, the harder the task of a satisfactory return to motion and the ungrudging reimmersion in the illusion."

Sam submitted a copy of this paper with his (entirely speculative) letter of application to Walt Disney Imagineering in Glendale, California. This was spring ninety-one, a year and a half into what they were calling there the Disney Decade, the decade, said the company chairman, when the "Disney Experience" was to be reinvented worldwide. After years of being dismissed as irredeemably hick by the so-called hip and intellectual, Disney was *relevant* again. You only had to watch the cream of the nation's architects vying to work on new projects to see the truth of that.

Invited to California for interview, Sam showed himself to have a perfect understanding of the relationship between the Disney worlds and the world that lay beyond the gates – their simultaneous convergence and divergence – crossing from one to the other in conversation without a trace of confusion or lag. He spoke knowledgeably and excitedly about fourth-generation technology and said that the invention that most intrigued him was the simple lock and key.

He was hired, and three months later was on a plane overseas to France.

It was late August, the temperature high 80s, when he arrived in Marne-la-Vallée. Nothing he had seen (in California, on his trips to Florida), nothing he had read (and in his short time at Disney he had read much) could have prepared him for what he found that first day he reported for duty: the scale of the construction, the profusion of ideas, the sheer physical endeavour. It was – easy to abuse the term, but nevertheless – little short of wondrous. Throughout the morning and afternoon, the roads in were thick with vehicles laden, like bearers of tribute from far-flung ends of empire, with trees and shrubs in leaf, with timber and stone and steel; and he asked himself what else, apart perhaps from war itself, could have mobilised so many men and machines.

(And these were the makers of the vehicles he saw along the road: Mercedes, Toyota, Renault, Volvo, Scania, Ford, M.A.N., Manitou, Caterpillar, John Deere, Hitachi, JCB. And these the contractors whose helmets the men wore: Pizzarotti, Nord-France, Phillip Holzmann, Taylor Woodrow, Grassetto, Docwra, Brophy, McGrew, Clancy of Harefield, Labour Only Construction Service . . .)

At one point in the afternoon he stood by the bare steel bones of the RER station, with, on one side of him, Frank Gehry's night-city strip beginning its climb away from the clay, watching as, on the other side, painters in cages turned the Disneyland hotel a soft, marshmallow pink. The road down to the park's entrances, lodged in arches under the hotel, wound gently round dry fountains, and trees, and an enormous banked flower-bed, soon to be planted with the trefoil shape of the famous Mouse-head. You couldn't have rushed it even if you had wanted to, and that, of course, was the whole idea: a gradual detachment from the run-of-the-mill, workaday world heightened the anticipation while at the same time ensuring that the new arrival did not succumb, by too quick an immersion in the fantastic, to the sensory bends.

It was, in its conception, quite perfect.

As he was walking back to the administration block a man in cycling shorts and a child's marshal's hat bounced by on a Kawasaki four-wheeled motorcycle. His buddy, riding pillion – backwards – smoked a cigar and scattered popcorn from a carton gripped between his thighs.

"My children," he said and made the sign of the cross. "My children, my children."

"It was like walking on to the set of M*A*S*H," Sam wrote his parents that night, thinking how much more likely they were to approve of that comparison.

Replaying the scene still later, though, in the last moments before sleep, the popcorn glittered like magic dust falling, and everywhere that it touched, it seemed something new, and wonderful to look at, sprouted.

Sam woke hungry for more. He couldn't get enough of it.

Right from the start, he made it his business to acquaint himself with every facet of the park's construction. He fell in with groups of workers walking to and from the site, chatting to them about their work, eating with them in their canteens; he became a familiar figure along the boomtown roads, always smiling, never lost for something to say – a polyglot of pleasantries. Even in the most casual encounter there was something to be learnt. He noted, for example, how matter-of-fact – how quickly – names such as Phantom Manor and Skull Rock sounded in the workers' conversations, like NASA in the mouth of a Houston Texan, or King of Prussia in a Philadelphian's. They were local landmarks, was all, prosaic places of work. But, if anything, this observation only added to the overall magic, for it proved just how real it had become for them. This was no mere amusement park, but the living and breathing thing Founder Walt had always intended it to be.

All this and more Sam committed to computer each night. He told his house-mate, Kent, that he felt it was important there was a record of some sort.

"Can you imagine if there had been a record of the building of, uh, the pyramids – the *Parthenon*, I mean like the sights and the sounds, the *smells* of the place? That's what I want to capture here."

Coming out of a meeting with a British contractor one afternoon (it was October, summer had turned to fall, heat haze to mist and rain, the dusty roads to quagmire), he called into the rest-rooms in their yard to take a leak. Beyond the locker room, two men stood rinsing their hands and arms over a trough brimming with brown water; the single urinal likewise brimmed, bright yellow. The handle had come off one of the two potties; the other still flushed, in theory, but was gagging on the sheer quantity it was being asked to swallow.

"Jesus Christ," Sam said, covering his nose. "What happened here?"

The men at the trough glanced over their shoulders to where Sam stood by the shower cubicles; the floors were awash, though with what exactly it was hard to determine. The men looked at each other, trying not to smile. Suddenly it seemed to Sam a preposterous question, his voice coming back to him childish and whining. He withdrew his pointing finger, turned, and hurried from the building.

In the car home that evening he suggested to Kent they eat dinner in Meaux, at a Lebanese restaurant they sometimes went to. They stayed on in town after their meal and had a couple of beers in a café on a bend in the river; more than a couple, maybe. Sam got a little drunk, it was really the only time he did. Kent was pretty sure there was something on his mind, but outside of work talk, and a single day-trip together to Paris, they were not especially close. He didn't know how to ask him.

"Everyone OK back home?" was the best he could do.

"Fine," Sam said, puzzled to be asked.

On the opposite bank street lights sent down fiery roots into the Marne.

"No, they're fine."

The following evening he was back at his computer.

It was not unusual for Kent to wake at two or three to go to the john and find his neighbour's lamp still lit, as it was indeed on the night before he disappeared. Asked about that night later Kent could only say Sam had seemed in very good spirits. They had talked a little at dinner, something about a book Sam had received a few days earlier, from the US, that he was interested in from the point of view of Sleeping Beauty's château. He did that a lot too, followed up sources, beyond what was strictly necessary, that is. (For weeks after he started at the Visionarium it had been anything connected with time travel and the Paris World's Fair.) He liked things in their proper context. He liked order.

He went straight to his room after he ate. Around midnight Kent heard from behind his door the fast flat patter of the computer keyboard. Again, this was not unusual.

After another week of damp November mists there was a real freeze-up that night, a sudden hard frost which thawed as quickly as it had fallen when the sun leaked through in the morning, turning the mud on site into a thick paste. It was one of those days (everyone working there knew them), things just *stuck*; as though the earth had decided on a whim to withhold its consent and make a human nonsense of the laws of motion. The air, when Sam arrived, was already heavy with the smell, frank as sweat, of diesel engines working flat out to drive wheels forward.

Down by Gate 4 a small crowd was gathered watching a Maniscopic forklift trying to lever a Belgian tipper truck out of a deep rut. As Sam drew level the forklift itself suddenly lost its purchase and reared up, scattering the spectators; a metal tine plunged over the front of the truck, precisely spearing the steering wheel. Just in time, the Belgian driver dove off, left, on to the grass, from where, plainly scared, he alternated between shouting at the forklift operator and nursing his ankle, twisted in the fall. The forklift operator shouted back in Spanish, scared himself. He tried to back up, but his own rear wheels had now become bogged down. The last Sam saw, looking back, the two vehicles were still locked in their weird embrace, like the tangled relics of an already ancient battle. The drivers, quiet now, communed on the sidelines in the lingua franca of a shared cigarette, relieved to have come out of it relatively unscathed.

This atmosphere of nervous caution appeared to have preceded Sam into the park itself. (There are definite moods to certain days, like viruses, instantly pandemic.) The smallest task was an effort, and as for anything more ambitious, the unspoken agreement seemed to be *why tempt fate?* In mid-morning Sam left the Visionarium where he had been running checks on the Timekeeper audioanimatron. He stopped beneath the nose of the Hyperion dirigible to exchange a few words with a colleague going into Video-polis. The colleague, knowing of Sam's interest in Disney colour, told him of a beauty of a conversation he had just overheard, two Irish guys – "Pat" and "Mick" – arguing at the edge of a trench.

Look at the state of that, Pat said. *What's wrong with it?* Mick asked. *It's not straight, that's what's wrong with it*, Pat said. *Listen*, said Mick, *all I was told was to dig a trench from here to there, nobody said anything about straight*.

Sam smiled on cue. He seemed cheerful enough, his colleague later reported. A little distracted, perhaps, but *it was one of those days*, nobody was quite themselves.

Sam excused himself, saying he had a message to do, and set off along the temporary road connecting Discoveryland with Fantasyland to the north-west.

Earth was piled eight or nine feet high at either side of the road, creating a kind of broad channel. There had been a heavy shower since Sam was last out and with that and the traffic there had been that morning the road surface was now more or less swamp. Sam kept his eyes on the ground much of the way, trying to stick to the shifting sidewalk of hardboard sheets, then looking up – feeling suddenly he *had* to look up – he noticed, as though he had just that moment been dropped there, a man, a West African, standing waist deep in mud, holding a section of wooden rainbow at full-stretch above his head. Sam tilted his own head a little, getting another angle, as if this was some kind of intentional exhibit he was looking at. The rainbow twitched (Sam's head twitched too) then seesawed wildly, buffeted by a sudden wind swirling between the walls of earth. The whole scene was instantly animated. The workman's hat tipped off on to his shoulder, his neck muscles tightened still further. His friends reached out to him from either side of the hole, calling to him to throw the rainbow section to them and pull himself free, but the foreman, a French guy, was yelling at them – had, perhaps, been yelling at them all along – and at the man in the hole that he was to do no such thing.

"Up! Up!" he kept saying.

The workman's arms flexed and locked. For a moment he

seemed to Sam to engage him in a stare that was close to disinterested, then his eyes closed, concentrating.

There was a sound in Sam's head, like the click of a fine key turning in a lock. White light flooded his brain wiping it clean of all its accumulated connections and responses. Almost at once, though, other, unfamiliar characters bubbled to the surface, formed incomprehensible words, which nevertheless became ideas of people and then images of them, joyously kinetic. It was a frigging *parade*, stretching back as far as he could think or see.

"Up! Up!" the foreman shouted.

Sam felt his feet move. He seemed to be walking in two planes simultaneously. He was marching beside the Big Parade still bubbling up in his head and he was wading through the gloop towards the foreman. The rainbow seesawed again, trailing the mud.

"Bastard! Shithead!"

The foreman swiped the air with his foot. The workman flinched, the rainbow dipped deeper into the mud, the foreman became apoplectic.

"Fired! Fired!"

He had his back to Sam so didn't see him closing in, reaching out a hand. Sam was telling himself he was only going to touch the man's shoulder, ask him to cool it. But, when the foreman unexpectedly spun round, Sam's out-stretched hand snatched at his throat while the other hand, tightened into a reflexive fist, came swinging over the top of his head like a club and slammed down on the upturned screaming face.

Whether it was the scream or the jarring impact that did it, Sam's double vision went at that moment and he recognised with absolute clarity where he was and what he was doing. Standing on a road between Discoveryland and Fantasy-land, holding a man in early middle-age by the throat. He glanced up at the turrets of the château – the hub, the big draw, the place towards which, in a roundabout way, he had been headed just now – then swung his fist again. He didn't connect properly the second time. The foreman slid out of his grasp on to the ground. He was shouting to the workmen to get help, he was shouting to Sam about the rainbow. Sam was kicking him.

"Fuck the rainbow! It's a hunk of fucking wood. You hear me? A hunk of fucking wood."

The foreman was dragging himself backwards on his elbows, Sam followed kicking him more. He was sweating and the meat of his hand was bleeding where he had caught the foreman's teeth, but he was doing OK. He was thinking if he could only get his hands on that hunk of wood he would kill this guy, but people were hurrying towards them by this time from other parts of the site and instead he turned and started to run. He scrambled up on to the railroad, slipping and falling flat on the ties, getting up and running again. He didn't even look to see if anyone was chasing him. All along the track-side men were wiring the embankments for spotlights or planting saplings. They watched, impassive, as Sam went past, beginning to hit his stride. He came into Main Street station like a runaway train, scattering the people working on the line, then careering off himself, down the skeletal station steps, across the plaza, and out through the central arch of the Disneyland hotel. No stopping, no looking back, neither to the left of him, nor to the right. He plunged straight through the flower-beds and cement fountains of Fantasia Gardens and on into the Marne countryside, lungs bursting with the cold air, head dizzy with adrenalin.

*

Some time in the early hours of the following day, Kent

Weinberger was woken by the telephone ringing in the kitchen of his shared apartment two miles from the town of Meaux. It was a few seconds before he remembered there was no one else home to answer it. He reached the receiver on the tenth ring.

"Sam? Where are you, guy? Are you OK?"

Actually, he sounded pretty far gone to Kent. You would have thought from the way he was rambling on that he had done something heroic the day before and not committed a serious felony.

"Sam, the police have gotten involved, they want to speak to you. The guy says you just came up behind and hit him."

At this point he became even harder to follow. He was talking about a rainbow falling in the mud; he mentioned a parade; he told Kent the witnesses would bear him out.

"But Sam," Kent said, "the witnesses all say the same thing as the foreman, far as I know. Sam?"

The embassy had already been notified. On their recommendation, and in the presence of one of their officials, the French police entered Sam's room that afternoon looking for clues to where he might be. They found none, found rather a perfectly orderly room, an almost *seminary* neatness, the only ornament Disney ornament. They found too the book he had sat up reading so late two nights before, a paperback practically snapped at the spine, furious scribbles in the margins and on the sheets of computer printout stacked on the desk and floor, one word leaping out – underlined, highlighted – from the rest: Berry, Berry, Berry, Berry. . .

Berry?

As a gesture towards its European setting, the castle at the far end of Main Street USA in Marne-la-Vallée is loosely based on the illustration of the Château de Saumur in *Les Très Riches Heures du duc de Berry*, an illuminated manuscript commissioned from the Limbourg brothers towards the close of the fourteenth century by Jean de Berry, brother of Charles V, King of France.

The duke was reputed to have had over twenty of these magnificently wrought Books of Hours in his vast personal library and seventeen castles – real, not illuminated – scattered about his lands in central and southern France. He had, in addition, some of the finest works of art in all of Christendom: sumptuous tapestries, triptychs bordered with precious stones. He had exquisite mosaics and marquetries, statuary that was the envy of all who saw it. He had a passion for dogs and had in his kennels breeds from every corner of the then known world. He had bears and swans and camels and apes, he had in short everything that fourteenth-century money could buy.

He had laxatives made from gold and pearls

He had the teeth of a narwhal

He had a tooth belonging to Charlemagne

He had a tooth recovered from the mouth of a giant

He had milk from the breast of the mother of Christ

He had hair from the head of the mother of Christ

He had Christ's own cup from the Last Supper

He had the sense of a gnat, the appetite of a goat, the discrimination of a dysfunctional magpie.

He had paintings started by one artist in one part of the country and finished by another artist in another part.

In middle age he had a wife of twelve.

He had to be removed as governor of Languedoc after tens of thousands of its inhabitants fled to Aragon to escape his outrageous taxes and arbitrary fines. But he had no shame whatsoever and carried on taxing and fining in his own territories of Auvergne and Berry. He had to in order to keep up the name he had acquired as the greatest collector of his day.

He had two brothers, Anjou and Burgundy, who ran him a close collective second, and a third brother, the King, who although abstemious by comparison nevertheless amassed enough in the way of riches and palaces in the course of his life to consider it wise as he lay on his deathbed to renounce the taxes that had provided them, the easier to slip through the needle's eye into Paradise.

He had cousins and in-laws in all the ruling houses of Europe and, when they weren't involved in squabbles over crowns, or plundering each other's territories, or besieging each other's cities, or holding each other to ransom, they attended banquets together at which upwards of thirty pairs of dishes were served, at which guests ate off gold and silver plate and gifts were exchanged: horses and gemstones and furs, the cream of their respective kingdoms.

By the time the duc de Berry died he had bled both his duchies dry.

He hadn't a sou to pay his debts. A pity, Sam thought, reading this, he hadn't lived today; he could always have opened his seventeen castles to the people he robbed, as theme parks.

```
┌─────────────┐
│             │
│    0220     │
│             │
└─────────────┘
```

Whistling, as instructed, "When You Wish Upon a Star",
heard half a minute before he is seen, a man, dressed at Sam's
direction only in shorts appears now at the point where the
rail track dips, standing pale against the shaft of blue-black
night. His right hand is pressed flat against the crown of his
head, his left, by his side, grips the handle of a red plastic
bucket. Sam calls on him to stop where he is and to turn
around through three hundred and sixty degrees. He does
this with some difficulty, barefoot on the rails. Black hair
glistens on his white shoulders as on his chest and stomach.
He is sweating and shivering, his penis in ribbed outline
against the shorts is drawn back on itself like a taut tuber.

"OK," Sam says.

The man comes on, stepping cautiously, his eyes all the
while on the trifid mass perched on the mountain ledge. His
manner is unaggressive, but his mouth now that he has
ceased whistling is a lipless furrow. Muscles prowl about
beneath the black body-hair, improbably contained. Sam
winds the blanket closer, winching in the heads either side of
him until they become one target with his own.

"That's far enough," he says, while the man is still some
way off.

The man sets the red plastic bucket on the ground, straightens and stares a moment, then about-faces and, whistling grimly, the same song as before, withdraws.

When he is satisfied that he really has gone, Sam unties Ilse Klein and lets her stand and make her shaky way along the track. She is in full view of him the whole time. When she arrives at the bucket she hangs her head, turns away, unable at first to do anything; but after so long sitting in the damp the pressure is too great. She gasps when her water begins, as though it was her shame itself she was passing, and for the first time tonight she appears to Sam to be in danger of losing all control.

Sam feels for her. He wishes things could be otherwise, truly he does. When he has tied her hands again he sees that her nose has been running. He takes a Kleenex from his pocket and wipes it for her. There is a moment then – her face turned towards him, balancing on his fingertips – when she is looking directly at him. Something is happening behind her eyes, a great personal battle is being fought. The lids twitch, dots and dashes relaying the struggle.

*

The shock of being kidnapped renders your will immobile. You become a sitting target, an accomplice to your own abduction. The kidnapper recognises and acts on this. If he says jump you jump, and when he says stop, you stop. The kidnapper always knows what you are going to do before you do, that is the advantage he has over you. You have your limit, you don't doubt, and you are demoralised each time you go beyond it.

The trickle in the bucket just now sounded to Ilse a cataclysm.

*

How is it possible to be grateful to someone for wiping your nose when he has made you squat before him over a bucket?

Because actually he is gentler than you had imagined and you are vulnerable to gentleness at that moment, even from him? Because your life with its store of memories is close to the surface all of a sudden and the act reminds you of other, past tendernesses? Because a person who goes to the trouble of cleaning your nose for you cannot be about to blow your head off?

The words come hard but she says them.

Thank you.

Because she was brought up to say them.

*

She was brought up in the Fifties, in a country divided rightside-leftside, like the hemispheres of the brain: a nuclear fission, cultivated difference weighed in megatons. She was brought up in a city pulling itself together, brick by brick, from the destruction of war. Rubble from the old Stuttgart was gathered into a monument overlooking the new. A television tower was erected, a symbol of the slow return to optimism and prosperity. Ilse grew up tall like her mother, with her mother's broad shoulders and long narrow feet. From her father she took a mouth inclined to smile and wide-set green eyes, from Konrad, a liking for climbing trees which she retained long after her brother had lost his. There were cherry trees along one side of the house where they settled in the Höhenlage from the tops of which Ilse could see over the wall into the grounds of the house next door. An old woman lived here alone. Frau Kepler kept her shutters closed summer and winter, and summer and winter wore the same black dress with an ankle-length sable coat for the one day in every month when she walked from her front door to the bottom of the steps where a taxi waited to take her to the bank. It was rumoured by the girls at Ilse's school that Frau Kepler was a millionairess. Some said she and her husband were Nazis and that her husband had been hanged after the war. They said her house was full of stolen treasure and lampshades made out of human skin. Others, however, said that Frau Kepler's husband had been killed by the Nazis themselves, that he was a hero and she a heroine.

When Ilse and Konrad were Old Enough To Understand, old enough, that is, to have begun to ask questions, their parents had sat them down together and explained to them about Hitler and the war. Children had first to try and imagine how it was in Germany in the years before the Nazis came to power, their father said: the depression, the dangerous instability. To begin with Hitler and his party had appeared as a gift from the heavens to many people. Ordinary decent people who wanted only to live in peace and have respect. When they were married themselves they would appreciate the strength of this desire and realise too that as a man or a woman your first duty was always to your husband or wife, before even your mother and father, and that when you had children they came before all other people – his voice faltered – all other people in the world.

Ilse glanced at Konrad, sullen behind his French fringe, building and collapsing steeples with his fingers. Their father cast about for words.

It was not as though anyone in this family had ever gone outside the law, their mother interjected, vexed: if ever they had been asked to do anything illegal they would not have accepted. When the law required their father to wear a uniform to work, he wore a uniform, and when it required him to go and fight, he went and fought, as simple as that. It was a bad time, nobody was pretending, but it was not obvious then what was obvious now, the things that were being done in their name. They did not know, until the war was over and they were shown the film by the American soldiers, about the camps, the death factories.

Later Ilse's father came to her room and sat on the bed without turning on the light. What their mother had told them, he said, was not quite true; there were occasions when he had feared what was to come, and he spoke to her of the *Kristallnacht* and waking to shattered glass swept into white drifts, for all the world like fallen blossom, before the gaping windows of Jewish businesses. People on the street that morning shook their heads, for shame, some hurried past holding their mouths as though afraid they would be contaminated by the transgression. Of course there were the gloaters, but even the Party appeared to distance itself a little. For a time things seemed almost to get better, or certainly not to get any worse, at least not here in Stuttgart, not in their neighbourhood; the yellow stars that you saw on television, stitched on to coats and dresses, those did not come until much later. Even after the war had begun some Jews were being allowed to leave the country. There was one family still living on the same street as Ilse's parents the summer of her father's call-up; sympathetic people in the town hall were trying to facilitate their emigration to the very last. And then, like that, they were gone, and no one could say what had become of the family.

But even then . . .

You cannot think the unthinkable, only afterwards, when it has been presented to you in all its irrefutable detail, and then sometimes you can think of nothing else.

He sat for a few moments in the darkness, then the bed creaked and he leaned over and kissed her head and she felt the fall of his empty sleeve on her pillow.

Frau Kepler died. The hearse came and her body was put into it and removers came and in the course of a single afternoon emptied the house of its contentious contents and locked the doors. Ilse was fourteen. She watched the brusque obsequies from the cherry trees, lying along a bough with her feet resting against the trunk and her chin hooked over the crotch of two branches separating; wedged tight as a bolt in a crossbow trained on the old woman's house. She kept it under surveillance for two days to see if anyone would come back; and when no one appeared, on the third day she went over the wall and broke in without difficulty through the kitchen window.

What was she expecting to find? Clues? *Skeletons?* She found only small things, hairpins, tin-tacks, rubber bands. The villa otherwise was entirely bare. Her footsteps ran all over the house while she did no more than walk down the hallway and into the drawing room. Everywhere the wooden floors bore the imprint of the recently removed furnishings, like markings made on a stage to show the exact position of the props: here the lamps, and here the carpet, and downstage right a sofa.

In that instant it was as though a light had come on inside her head and she saw with perfect clarity what life became with age, a shrinking repertoire of entrances and exits – church on Sunday, work on Monday, friends on Saturday, dinner at eight, from week to week, from year to year, from altar to grave. She pictured the entire city marked out in this way and in every apartment, in every house, no matter how big, the same limited moves being made. She realised too the true crime of her parents all through the war years in simply turning up for work on time, or waiting in orderly line to collect their rations. Stuttgart then seemed to her more at risk from these thoughts than ever it had been from the enemy air-raids. What was that anyway, *Stuttgart?* It appeared to quake beneath the scrutiny, as though all that was needed was for a few more people to question it and the whole city would simply crumble once and for all into dust.

She mounted the stairs, serene in the power of her youth and intuition, the shine returning to the banister beneath her hand, like velvet righted. There were, as she had anticipated, circles on the shelves in the bathroom cabinet indicating exactly where the medicines and toiletries were to be placed, there was even a mark, a yellow outline, on the bath's white porcelain for the water to aim at when the tap was turned on. This precise life, accounted for down to the very last drop.

She sat on the toilet kicking her feet on the linoleum, humming, happy beyond reason. Presently she became conscious of a bunching between her hips. She let it grow more insistent then she stood and undid her slacks and sat down again, concentrating. In a few moments she felt her rectum dilate and with great deliberation her bowels delivered a single elliptical shit, a honey-coloured bomb, into the inverse city of the sewers.

She remembered this moment ten years later in Berlin, when in a villa lent for the day on an island in the Wannsee, white drapes bubbling in the yawning windows, she crouched, anus open, above an upright penis and for the third time watered it with her piss, watching detached as the glans finally ripened and split like a purple fruit and sent its bleached seed fluttering into the whirring klieg-lit air.

0228

Ilse is contemplating these two images of herself – searching for a geometry that can express the distance between them, and the distances between each one and here, Big Thunder Mountain, the third point of this bizarre biographical triangle – when a hand shutters her eyes and blots out the light and it is once again black night.

*

The way Raymond is sitting all he gets of the man bringing the bucket is the soundtrack: the precise instructions, the whistling, and the shouted commands and then a little later the intimate hiss of Ilse Klein urinating. When she has returned to the ledge and her hands have been retied she says thank you, her tee-aitch very faintly sibilant. For a long while nothing else happens. Raymond begins to think his turn is never going to come, and then just when he is least expecting it, though with hindsight he sees he ought to have expected it precisely then, the blanket is loosened and Sam is urging him to get to his feet. He stands, his legs buckle, he sits. Sam helps him up again and unties his hands.

"Stamp your feet," he says, but Raymond's feet feel heavy and improbable and the mechanics of stamping are far beyond him.

He shuffles forward, head bowed. His trousers are corrugated stiff with sweat and the creases chafe at the backs of his knees when he moves. Inside the legs themselves, however, the blood at last begins to flow again, a thick warming liquor. His ice-block feet prickle with life return-ing. He throws one foot forward speculatively and is heartened by its solid impact. He throws the other one, and then the first one again, and so on, clown-walking down the track to the bucket. He is starting to feel a little more like himself, even going to the toilet, beyond the initial rush of embarrassment, is a kind of reaffirmation, and he is reminded then of the small release of prison mornings, that momentary expansion, like a deep inhalation, of the possible universe before the multiple confinements of the prison day descend again to stifle you. Without such fleeting illusions, he thinks, even knowing that illusions are all they are, you would not survive there for very long.

He takes his time doing up his fly, putting off the moment of return, and, why he doesn't know, other than it's where he is after all and names are anchors of a sort, says the word *France* quietly to himself. The letters seem almost to leap before his mind's eye as his mouth forms them, a mental voiceprint which fades with the slight sound of the word itself, its pattern of peaks succeeded by an image, postcard-clear, of the cathedral at Meaux and the derelict swifts' nests he had seen growing like goitres from the stone throats of the figures carved above the ancient double doors. It comes back to him with all its original force the strangeness of arriving in a place that was nowhere you had ever heard of to find that history had been going about its business for the best part of a millennium undeterred by the lack of interest. The very birds' nests looked like monuments. And the continent had barely begun to get into its stride: for hundreds of miles to the north and south and hundreds more to the east, fanning out into the continents beyond, towns and cities, large and small, busied themselves with their corporate lives; Meaux upon Meaux upon Meaux, all the villes and burgs and grads and stadts that crowded the maps. . . He had the feeling that day he had as a child, crossing Belfast by bus on winter evenings, squeezed between his mother and the window, watching as people got off and walked up streets he didn't know, lit by lampposts hung, perhaps, with the swings of other children, their initials scored on the side with the point of a chalky hopscotch stone. The city had seemed such a generous place that it could accommodate so much life. Later, when he was thirteen and stricken for the sixth successive school year with streaming sinuses, his mother had taken him to the hospital to be tested for allergies. Behind a curtain in a cubicle, off a long sepia corridor, a grid was drawn on his forearm and the centre of each tiny square pricked with a potential irritant. After an interval bumps began to appear, an erratic pattern of reaction. The doctor noted it down as noughts and crosses, ringing the largest bumps with purple ink, before moving on to the next cubicle. Raymond heard the murmured conversation and from further down the corridor other voices, coughs, a toddler crying. All those people sitting behind the curtains each with their unique flag on their arm. . . He burned with something he could not understand, but thought must be sadness because it made him want to cry. (It was not until many years afterwards, when the first photograph of May holding the baby was brought to him in his cell, that he recognised this feeling for what it was, which was love.) It was 1967, the globe was contracting under the all-seeing eye of the satellite, but Belfast was still world enough for him.

There was, though, another darker thought associated in Raymond's mind with the town of Meaux and its cathedral's slow decay into nature. His Grandfather Milligan, his mother's father, born on a farm in county Armagh, had fought in the blasted woods and fields of the Somme in the Great War and had come home to Ireland a convert to concrete. He moved up to Belfast, found a job with a firm of asphalters and stayed there forty-five years. He saw out his retirement, a contented widower, in a block of flats in the cement heart of the Braniel estate. Towards the end, though, the days began to be told off in bombs. Belfast was coming down around him. He ventured into the centre of town only once after the bombers moved in, with Raymond and his father, to be measured for a suit for a wedding he would never attend. In fact, he got no closer to the hire shop that day than the corner of Queen Street where he stopped, staring down into a great muddy hole where once a shop had stood. Seagulls, perched on tumbled cliffs of masonry, looked up at him from their reclaimed watery domain.

Grandfather Milligan couldn't go another step. He began to cry, old man's tears, a silent dampness irrigating the entire expanse of his face.

"No more," he said.

Raymond and his father took him back to the flat, five flights up, where he died, five months later, without having set foot on the street again. It frightened him, he told his grandson, to be reminded of what lay so close to the surface. If he'd been a younger man, he told him too, he would have gone out with a gun and found the people responsible. Don't think he wouldn't. (Those last months his every second sentence was to defend the one before it from imagined slight.) He'd done it before, hadn't he? And there was no point telling him it wasn't part of the same war.

There were plenty of old men like him back then and plenty of young men like Raymond hanging on to their words.

*

We are, of course, talking nano-seconds here. From mountain to Meaux, to Belfast and back again. So, Raymond finishes doing up his fly and turns around and sees as before the backpack lying on the track and, to the right and beyond it, Sam gazing at him steadily. He has covered Ilse Klein's eyes with one hand, though whether out of some belated notion of propriety or to stop Raymond and her exchanging glances, Raymond can't begin to guess. Her head is bent forward, unresisting, towards her knees. Raymond sees only the swirl of her hair where it seems to drain off-centre into the crown, her thick flecked hiking socks and ankle-high trainers.

Sam's other hand maintains a firm grip on the gun, tracking Raymond's every step. His lips, Raymond notices, never stop moving. He puts Raymond in mind of something, a squirrel, maybe, nibbling a nut, or, better yet, of a wee lad he used to play football with who commentated to himself non-stop under his breath, as though he needed to hear the story told before he could believe in it. His lips move but the sounds that fall from them are barely audible, husks of words, gnawed to nothing. Tiny fragments flake all the while from around the mouth of his tight cracked mask of mud. Raymond wonders that he has not realised the significance of this mask before now. One of Ollie Thompson's favourite sayings (Ollie Mark 2, that is, the Ollie of the entrenched coat and the breadless pieces):

"A mask is your something and your something else."

Your *defence* and your what? – absolution? No, too confessional sounding for Ollie – *exoneration*, that was it. Masked you ceased to be Ollie Thompson, or Raymond Black; masked you became the faceless instrument of your cause. Ollie said.

Looked at this way, Raymond has no difficulty accepting Sam's claims that someone, or something, else is acting through him, that he is performing lines that have been scripted for him by another hand. He sees through the gaps in the tracks an errant beam picking its way over the builders' jumble below. The light touches the discarded objects with a sort of reverence, as though they were treasures it had stumbled upon, making unfamiliar icons of an inverted Pot Noodle and a Coke can studded with butts. He wavers for a moment on the verge of a deeper under-standing, then the other spotlight catches his eye, flitting suddenly across the wall, ringing Sam round with a corona of brightness, and Raymond gasps in recognition and pulls in his head. . .

"Hey, what the fuck? Are you OK?"

Before Sam's very eyes the Irish guy has just shrivelled, from one moment to the next, to three-quarters – two-thirds – *half* his original size. His clothes seem to follow a split second out of sync, collapsing inwards. The lights are suddenly zooming all around. Sam suspects some gross cine-graphic metamorphosis and almost forgets himself so far as to stand up unprotected.

"Fucking cut it out, Ray."

Raymond blinks, eyes and body both. He discovers he has gone into a deep crouch, hands closed in startled fists, right leg, raised a little off the ground, drawn across the left. He looks down at himself and then looks up. The black hole in the dry brown oval is Sam's mouth hanging open. Raymond understands, he has surprised himself. He gives a little shrug, straightening, and it seems to Sam as if he is pumping himself back up into his jacket.

"Jesus Christ, man, that was frigging scary."

Sam has taken his hand away from Ilse's face. She swivels her forehead on her knee, enough to peek out with one open eye. She winks it at Raymond. He twitches his own. He needs to sit again. His hands are tied and the blanket is passed under his chin.

"Thank you," he says.

*

Sometimes Raymond remembered what it was he had done. He never forgot completely, but mostly the memory of it bobbed, like a balloon on a mile-long string, on the outer limits of his consciousness, only distantly connected to him. At other times, though, the balloon turned without warning to lead and plummeted in on him. He would flinch, sensing it coming, but too late. It entered his brain as a thudding pain, forced its way past his contracting throat, choking it of air, and crashed through his chest and stomach to his bowels, so that only the spasmodic tensing of his buttocks saved him from shitting himself in shamed surprise. He might be standing beside someone, a total stranger, shoulder to shoulder, watching football at a bar, or buying apples and oranges from a man in a shop where he had never been, their four hands – crossing in the two-way traffic of fruit and money – touching, and he would duck inside as the question hit home: *him?* could it have been this man? And sometimes in his dreams everything went as planned that night in the car with Gillespie and Ollie Thompson and he parked in a street where children were playing hopscotch with a white stone on the black footpath and he watched in the mirror as Ollie got out and walked to the door. And the man who answered his knock might be the man who had stood beside Raymond in the bar, who had turned to him after their striker had missed one absolute sitter and said, commiserating, *Pockle*, or he might be the greengrocer, and he would try to close the door, knowing what was coming and knowing too that he had let himself in for it by serving Raymond apples and oranges, or saying Pockle like that when the striker ballooned the ball over the crossbar; never mind Ollie in his mask that meant to say don't take this personally. . .

0330

In Fort Collins, Colorado, it is 9.30pm. The town is draped with yellow ribbons. On car aerials, door knockers, trees of course, old oaks, young birch, whatever. Yards and yards and yards of yellow ribbons. Neighbours and strangers alike shake one another by the hand. Television channels coast to coast broadcast the pictures. A man in a yellow tie shakes the hand of one of the many interviewers who prowl the sidewalks. Invited to say a few words, he looks right into the camera, right out of a zillion TV sets, red-faced with joy.

"Welcome back, Tom," he says.

"Ladies and gentlemen, the voice of Fort Collins – the voice of *America* – tonight," the interviewer says, putting himself between the man and the camera.

Fireworks explode somewhere close by, the interviewer ducks, looks over his shoulder, looks back, grins.

"Welcome back, Tom!"

A rocket explodes in Vukovar. The town has fallen, but fighting continues around the hospital. What clocks remain there show all sorts of crazy times. Some show hours without the minutes, others minutes without the hours, still others show nothing but blank inarticulate faces. The uncertainty is forgivable. On the ground (*under* the ground, in cellars and in bunkers) besieged citizens – Croats, Serbs, Hungarians, Ruthenes, and every cross-fertilisation imaginable – adopt the tactics of besieged citizens since urban time began. Heads down and hope.

*

Sam has asked four times now for the man in shorts, the Whistler, to come back and remove the bucket. He explains to Ilse and Raymond that he is sensitive to the smell of other people's urine (no offence). He tells them about the toilets he went into in one of the contractors' lots. (He has told them this, as he has told them a good deal else, at least once already tonight, as if his stories are on a random loop.) He tries the radio again. Oh, this is great. Now Gary is not there, Gary is resting. They all have cots rigged up in the Silver Spur Steakhouse, the new guy, Reuben, says: real warm and comfortable. Sam asks about the bucket. What bucket's that? Reuben asks him. Gary didn't mention any bucket to him. He asks someone over his shoulder. Nope, they say, nor them. He says he'll find out what's what. Five minutes later, still no word, Sam is back on the radio to him. Reuben says another five minutes, Sam waits six or seven and tries again. This goes on. He is not angry, Ilse thinks, but baffled. It seems such a little thing to cause all this fuss when there have been so many big things set in train this night. At last Reuben says there's someone on the way. Yeah, Sam says, and not before time, but the words strain for conviction. Ten minutes later and the bucket's still sitting there. Now Sam is beginning to get impatient. At one point he even puts the radio first to Ilse's mouth, then to Raymond's, *Here, you tell him*, but then thinks better of it and next time he speaks there's Gary again answering. Thank God you're back, Sam says. That frigging Reuben! Gary commiserates with him. Yeah, Reuben.

Almost immediately the whistling starts up far down the track.

More and more now, the minutiae of causality matter to Sam. The accumulation of incidental detail proves that things could not have been other; each stray word, each scrap of fact, is a witness for his defence. He would be a junkman of derivations, an archaeologist dusting down the mute fragments of experience, giving them context and voice. He would be Sam the Human Computer committing to memory the chronologies of his companions' lives, cross-referencing them with his own. Pick a day, he would say, any day. Yesterday? The day before? Too easy. Yesterday, the day before *last year*, five or six years ago – eight, ten, any number you care to name: eight *and* ten even.

Eighteen years ago, then.

See this moment already in train!

*

Maine, Fall 1973

Jennifer sits at the kitchen table, wiping under her eyes with the knuckles of her index fingers. The tears, diverted, follow her jawline until they are atomised by the L of blonde hairs at the hinge. Tom at the stove makes a big pot of coffee spooning half a dozen granular mountains from the instant coffee jar and pouring in water hot but not boiling from the kettle. Pour then stop, pour then stop, pour then stop: One, his mouth says, two, three. . . A sweet sappy smell comes off the stove fire where the first logs from the cord of wood delivered the day before are burning to an accompaniment of pops and tweets.

It is raining out, hard. The gutters are bubbling over and pools have formed in the folds of the tarpaulin thrown over Arnold Woolf's Chrysler. Arnold was working at the engine again this morning. After breakfast, while the weather was still fine, Sam joined the other kids out front, sitting on a fence to watch Arnold spread his oily sheet on the ground, raise the hood and peer inside. He stayed down today for longer than it took Martha Gibbons to count to four hundred – the cuffs of his coverall riding up the further into the engine he reached, revealing more and more of his grey pant legs – then came up holding in his rag a plug coated in grease. Arnold's Chrysler had not started for as long as anyone living there could remember. Sometimes, with coaxing, the engine would growl a bit, the way an old dog might, Tom said, more to encourage its owner than out of any real conviction, but it could never sustain the vigour for long and soon the growl would falter to a cough, the cough to a splutter, then the splutter would wheeze into silence. But still, every Saturday morning, without fail, Arnold could be seen bent under the hood tapping and wrenching. There was barely a part of the engine that he had not had out on the sheet by this stage. The children who gathered to watch sat on the fence and on the ground, chins on knees, making fat lips, as each piece was cleaned or discarded and replaced.

"Is that it this time?" they called to Arnold.

Arnold would frown, wiping his hands on the rag, and come round slowly to the driver's seat and turn the key.

This morning, like every other morning, he got out of the car a few moments later, unsuccessful, and folded the sheet away for another week.

Tom rattles the lid of the coffee pot. The lid is dented and only Holly knows how to fit it into the neck of the pot without struggling. Jennifer is chain-smoking, though Jennifer does not normally smoke at all. She gets real drama into lighting and crushing the cigarettes, but in between seems content to let them smoulder in the ashtray. She wipes her eyes again.

Something, the look on his mother's face perhaps – several stages back from real concern – makes Sam think that this has happened before, or will happen again, or is at any rate a part of a far larger happening.

Holly holds a sheet of paper at arm's length on the red Formica tabletop. Sam climbs up, almost too big these days for her lap, and leans his elbows on the table between hers. He is four and a half now and having to get to grips with the world as it is written. He recognises all of his letters and can make with them the names of the animals whose sounds were his first acquired speech acts, dog cat cow goat hen.

"That was on the bed when I got back," Jennifer says.

Sam studies it, his eyebrows warping with the effort to understand. It is more like drawing than writing. A box of letters with no spaces between them, its borders red and red the line snaking through it.

Tom sets the coffee pot on the table and eases the sheet of paper from Holly's hands, which don't move, Sam notices, as does Tom who smiles in that secret way he has that does not use his mouth. Sam squirms down from Holly's knees and moves round on to his father's and tries again with the word box. It is no good, though. Jennifer lights a cigarette, a blade of flame and a rush of smoke. Sam's attention wanders to the window and suddenly he sees it – the letters on the page – slanting across the glass and without knowing what any of it means he understands that Jen has run away.

mainemainemainemainemainemainemainemainemaine
arainrainrainrainrainrainrainrainrainrainrainrainn
iinrainrainrainrainrainrainrainrainrainrainrainrainraii
nnrainrainrainrainrainrainrainrainrainrainrainrainraina
erainrainrainrainrainrainrainrainrainrainrainrainrainrm
mainrainrainrainrainrainrainrainrainrainrainrainraine
arainrainrainrainrainrainrainrainrainrainrainrainrainrn
iainrainrainrainrainrainrainrainrainrainrainrainrainrai
nnrainrainrainrainrainrainrainrainrainrainrainrainraina
einrainrainrainrainrainrainrainrainrainrainrainrainraim
mnrainrainrainrainrainrainrainrainrainrainrainrainraie
arainrainrainrainrainrainrainrainrainrainrainrainrain
inrainrainrainrainrainrainrainrainrainrainrainrainrai
nrainrainrainrainrainrainrainrainrainrainrainrainra
eainrainrainrainrainrainrainrainrainrainrainrainrainram
minrainrainrainrainrainrainrainrainrainrainrainraie
anrainrainrainrainrainrainrainrainrainrainrainrainran
iinrainrainrainrainrainrainrainrainrainrainrainrainraii
nnrainrainrainrainrainrainrainrainrainrainrainrainraina
emainemainemainemainemainemanemainemainemaine *maim*

Arnold stands at his window across the lot, watching the water gather on the tarpaulin.

More than anything in the wide world at that moment Sam wants to be the one who looks under the hood of Arnold's car and finds the part that makes everything OK.

*

Coming out of Lisburn there now, climbing up Chapel Hill on to the Longstone, seen Davy Chambers leaving the Niagara with a big bag of chips. Banged the window, but Davy'd on him a Linfield monkey hat pulled down over his ears and never heard me. Chips at this time of the morning. *You Fat Bastard, Chambers.*

Old Warren. The bus stops facing the shops. Women getting on with trolleys and babies. No change any of them, of course, and fourteen bags to search through before they find their purse. Man beside me picks his teeth with his rolled-up ticket. The smoke from the back seats is wild, like a second ceiling near, or like a veil everyone has to walk through getting on or off. Wee girl sits down with a Tiny Tears across the way and starts hoking at its nappy to see if it's wet. Her ma gives her a welt on the hand. Don't Do That On The Bus.

Old Warren. Always reminds me of the tramp I saw that time, somewhere round here, with a lame dog trussed up on a go-kart. Legs at the front, wheels at the back. Flipping wild.

Moving again, about time. Flaming seats are hard on the auld arse, boy. The back of the one in front's covered in black circles where fags have been stubbed out on the red vinyl. There are helmets of ash on the windowsill. They roll down the rubber gutter towards me when we're going up a slope, then bomb back the other way when we start to go down again. Burn House, Hull's Hill Mission Hall, Maghaberry, back and forward they roll, then jitter on the spot as the road straightens out between two huge flat fields.

(Is that where this is, Flatfield?)

The fields are a brown mess after the harvest. *Turned over.* You say it like that it sounds like looting. Wonder if. . . Nah, it's daft, soil's soil, it can't feel anything. All the same, if you imagine the cauliflowers or whatever like teeth being pulled out. . . No Thank You.

Moira. Prod. Couple of big country lads get on, Noddy Holder sideburns. Shite all over their shoes. The bus is just about full now: standing room only. The windows mist up in patches with the breath from forty-odd mouths. The glass squeaks under my sleeve when I wipe it.

Everyone's gone dead quiet all of a sudden. Flipping brilliant when that happens. Just the engine sound and people smacking their papers straight. Counted two *Irish Newse*s when I was getting on. Three *News Letter*s. Three to two to us. *Ee-ea-sy!* A heap of *Sun*s and *Mirror*s too, like, but you can't tell with them one way or the other.

Lurgan police station got it last night. Car bomb. It's on all the front pages. My da says this morning, Watch you yourself going down there. (Like as if there was no trouble in Belfast.) I should have said to him, *Going's* the easy part. It's coming back scares me. It's true, though, that last bus, stopping off at all those estates. One night in the summer, outside Lurgan, a fella in a combat jacket stepped out from the scrub at the side of the road carrying a rifle. He watched the bus as it went past then crossed over to the other side and jumped the hedge into a field. Some woman started shouting at the bus driver to drive to the cop shop. Missus, are you wise? the driver shouted back. I have to work this route five nights a week, I've a wee family to think of.

It wasn't right, but. You couldn't just let them walk about like they owned the place. May says what's new, half the estates in Craigavon are crawling with Provies and the cops do nothing. May and her family were put out of their house in Belfast a couple of summers back, before I met her. She says her Catholic neighbours stood by and clapped as they loaded up the van. Tony, May's da, chucked a can of paraffin up the walls of the front room and threw a match on it. If I'm not going to be let live in this house, he said, I'm damned sure I'm letting nobody else.

Bus pulls up again. Magheralin. In and out. *Macra*lin or *Mara*lin? Never know. May says Macra. Is it us says Macra and them says Mara? Like spell Harry. Say haitch-ah up our way and you're fucked.

The big country lads are moving forward to get off. Where do you go on a Saturday morning one stop out of Magheralin? All's there is is a row of cottages beside the bus sign then nothing but fields way down to Donaghcloney. Flipping lovely looking, though, sometimes, the country-side. Be great getting out somewhere you didn't know and just walking. Thought about that sort of thing a couple of times lately, even baling out altogether, going to England maybe. Scotland'd be better. May says no way (May says no way to most things), if you go you're on your own. Thought about that too a couple of times. Why not after all? I'm still only twenty, I'm not old yet.

There's something white fluttering in a hedge out the other window. I have to blink at it a few times, the way you do when you wake up in the night and can't remember who you are. The man sitting next to me has chewed one end of his ticket to a pulp and stuck it to the back of the seat in front. The rest of the ticket's rolled up tight and sticking out like an erection. The something white in the hedge has red and blue in it too. A Vanguard flag. Should have guessed. Ollie Thompson wore his like a cape at the rally that time last year in Lisburn, the night he shook Bill Craig's hand. The Leader! he was shouting, full as a po. I shook hands with the Leader! There were wee fellas shaking hands with Ollie just on the strength of it.

Follow, follow, we will follow Bill Craig,
Up the Falls, Derry's walls, we will follow on.
Follow, follow, we will follow Bill Craig,
If he goes to Dublin we will follow on.

But that was last year. Ollie Thompson said he wouldn't walk to the end of the street to see that man now. Where was Bill Craig when the army were beating down doors and lifting the people who had marched for him? Up there at the end of that big drive of his out of harm's way.

Bill Craig, Ollie Thompson said, was a wanker like all the rest. Takes one to know one, Ollie, May said.

The road bends right then left then there's another flag, a Union Jack, flying from the top of a big white pole behind a war memorial. Dollingstown. Grey houses, red poppies. Staunch. A girl with feathered hair gets on wearing a tartan scarf round her wrist. Half, she says, daring the driver to challenge her, to Craigavon Centre. Her face is as white as bread. She takes the ticket and looks down the bus at the rest of us: *See enough?*

Millie, May would say. (Funny word, Millie: hard woman and easy girl, the way May means it.) She takes the outside seat in front of me. Big waft of patchouli oil and cherries and the vodka-y smell of hairspray. The chewed ticket hard-on sticks out from the back of her seat. I feel my own dick unravel in my Ys. The Millie stuffs an Anglo bubbly in her mouth and leans across and chucks the old one out the sliding window. I'm up a boner now. An instant bus boner, cold, tight and uncomfortable. If I move the man next to me'll notice it for sure. Look out the window. Think about something else: sausages, Gillespie always says, then waits for you to tell him to wise up, sausages would remind you of what you were trying to forget – *Frying?* he asks.

The tip of the Millie's tongue pokes out, sheathed in pink:

once, twice, three times, then her tongue disappears and the cheek nearest me bulges and as the bulge subsides a bubble starts to grow. Her cheek bulges again and again; the bubble keeps on growing from between her wet lips. (*The stale smoky smell of Cookeen melting in the fry pan. Twist the sausages and cut their cords. Drop them in, blistering and spitting.*) The bubble is huge. Her nose is resting on the top, denting it. The rest of the bubble is straining to see-through where the air is pushing to get out. (*The sausage splits lengthways, saturated with hot lard, gristly insides still half raw, underside burnt black: black burnt pig flesh.*) The bubble bursts, so that for a moment in the air before her face you can nearly see where it isn't. Where it is is all over her chin and top lip. The Millie's tongue darts about winding in the tattered pieces and flicking them back into her mouth.

Lurgan.

The police station's wrecked all right. Bastards.

The bus three-quarters empties, then starts to fill again. The man next to me goes. I stretch my legs out, reach into my pocket, like I'm looking for a hanky or change, and just have time to rearrange my dick before a big skinhead swings into the empty seat. I hold on to my dick. *It won't go down.* If the skinhead sees it he'll fucking kill me. *May* will fucking kill me if I get off the bus in this state.

See you, that's all you ever think about. Well you're not coming into our house with it like that.

Well help me then, May.

Fuck away off and do whatever it is you fellas normally do.

May says it like she doesn't know what it is we do do. But May knows. She's slipped the hand on me dozens of times before now. Neither of us lets on she's doing it. She wraps her fingers around me, pulling down the skin, touching the head with her thumb. She rubs gently. If I come she wipes her hand on my stomach and, if we're in the house, goes off up to the bathroom. Once, when she was rubbing me, without saying anything, she took my hand and put it between her legs. I cupped the lump in her tights. She breathed out like she'd been punched, but when I pulled away she held my hand by the wrist. No, she said, really quiet, almost as if she wasn't talking to me. Her tights were wet. I felt inside them, inside her knickers. Her stomach made two long folds then there was hair in tight, flat curls. The hair was dry as leaves and beneath it there seemed to be nothing but bone. I moved my fingers further down, not knowing what else to do. I felt her legs open wider. The curls got damper, the flesh behind them softer, but even then nothing I touched seemed to lead anywhere. I couldn't believe how far down I had to go before the actual *fanniness* of her fanny began. And how sudden it was. My finger sank in up to the knuckle, she shifted a bit and another finger got drawn in behind it. I was feeling all around her, not in a horny way, just in a surprised way. I wondered how long she'd been like this. I wondered was she like this at other times, when we watched TV, when we were sitting somewhere having a drink. How would you know?

Ow, she said. I was touching something I shouldn't have been. She had me rubbed sore. I'd forgotten what she was doing. The adverts were on, we just sort of stopped, took our hands back. We both had red rings on our wrists from each other's waistbands.

If Tony had come home then and seen them he'd have had my balls off.

The bus is looping round the Craigavon estates. The skinhead gets up abruptly and jams his thumb against the bell running along the ceiling. The driver sets him down in a lay-by above an underpass. As the bus pulls out again, the skinhead shoots a filthy look at me. I go to turn away, then I realise it's not me he's looking at at all, but the Millie. The

Millie's staring straight back at him, without even seeming to see him. She blows another bubble. It snaps like old elastic. She has a glance at her watch (the strap is massive, three buckles, red plastic wet-look): quarter to twelve. Wonder is she meeting someone? Wonder is she wet down there. The secret life of Fanny and Dick, stories by the busload.

Eeesshh!

Flipping tatt's itching. Rub my arm against the seat. No good, can't scratch it through this coat. Drive you flipping mad sometimes. May hates it. It's not even a proper Union Jack, she says. It's just a square with four lines in it. That's cause we done them ourselves. It was like a mass dare, one night last summer when the crowd of us were guarding the bonfire. You had to do it, you couldn't lop out.

And, May says, it's *green*. That was Ollie, it was him got the ink and, right enough, it looked blue in the bottle.

May's da has a cracker Union Jack on his shoulder, you can make out all three crosses. When he flexes his muscles it even looks like it's fluttering. May says he has a mermaid on his right calf and when she was young she used to roll up his trouser-leg to look at it while he was standing at the sink shaving.

He's not that old, May's da. He was a real Ted when her ma met him. Still wears the winkle-pickers and his hair all greased back. Ollie says a mate of his up the top of the Woodvale knows him. Ollie says his mate up the top of the Woodvale is in the UVF. Ollie says he showed him his piece one day at work. (Ollie makes it sound like a roast-meat sandwich.) Fucking beautiful thing, Ollie says. Ollie and guns. When Ollie says 45 these days you can bet it's not a record he's talking about. I asked him one night, down at the snooker hall, Ollie are you in anything? He rolled his shoulders inside his trench coat (the entrenched coat, as May calls it: he never has it off his back), Maybe I am, he said, and maybe I'm not. *No*, in other words, I think. The way things are, it's hard to tell for sure, even with people you grew up with. Mind you, it's hard sometimes to remember things ever being any other way. Ollie the hippie, hanging round outside the Linen Hall on Saturday afternoons when he was fifteen with a tie round his bap and his ma's sheepskin coat on him, looking to buy grass, coming home with a wee packet of silver paper some fella had sold him for a quid. There were five of us – Ollie, me, Sharon, Clare Mooney, and what's-his-name, Jeff, Sharon's brother – in Ollie's bedroom, one of Ollie's records on that's three seconds of singing and twenty minutes of guitars. He unwraps the stuff. We all look at it. Browny-black flakes in the bottom of the packet. Is that what it's supposed to look like? Clare says. Ollie swirls it with his finger. Course, he says. He makes a complicated criss-cross of papers, mixes some of the browny-black flakes with tobacco and, with Sharon helping him hold up the ends, rolls it into a joint. (Even then they have to wind the gummed strips of two more papers around it to keep the thing from coming apart in the middle.) Ollie gets first smoke. Oh, he says, pulling his head back, then smoking again. Oh-OH! He has another couple of draws and holds it out to us, lying on his back. Sharon, Clare and I look at each other. (Sharon's brother, Jeff, is sniffing at the stuff in the tinfoil, jerking his head out of the road every time he gets any sort of a whiff of it.) I'm remembering stories about people winding up in Purdysburn after bad trips. Ollie's still holding the joint out to us. Sharon takes it, nervous, smokes with her eyes closed softly, like she's saying her prayers. Then opens them. I don't feel anything, she says. She smokes again, looks at the joint, shakes her head. Do you? she asks and gives it to Clare. (Jeff has his nose stuck right in the silver paper by this stage.) Clare takes a puff, coughs – Swallow it right, Sharon tells her – tries a second time, her face bulging as she struggles to keep the smoke down. She opens her mouth. Nothing, she says. I'm about to have a go myself when Sharon's brother looks up from the tinfoil. Do you know what this is? he says. Fucking Fyffes: Bonita Bananas. I smell the smoke coming from the end of the reefer. He's right. Oh-*OH!* Ollie says. His head's moving from side to side on the rug in – time's hardly the word – *reaction* to the guitar solo. Ollie, Sharon says and kicks his foot, it's flipping banana skins, but Ollie's smiling to himself, miles away.

When I asked him later how he could possibly have got high on banana skins he just shrugged. You've got to really want to, he said.

Ollie has bar-bells in his bedroom now. He has a ramp he built himself, against one of the walls, that he runs up and down while he's doing hand grips. He's getting himself into training, he says.

He's a lemon, May says.

Craigavon Shopping Centre! the driver shouts. The Millie runs her hands through her hair to feather it more. There's a guy waiting at the bus stop is the spit of one of the Faces. May's standing beside him. She waves from the elbow up when she sees me at the window. *Ping!* my dick pops up again. I pull my coat round so it's covering me. The queue to get off is taking for ever. I duck my head every few steps and shrug out the window. May's hopping from foot to foot, smiling. The Millie gets off a couple in front of me. The Faces fella is lighting two cigarettes and he hands her one and they walk off without a word to each other. May hasn't so much as glanced at them. I step out, feel the wind cut through my trouser-legs. May tilts her head for a kiss before I'm anywhere near her. The root of my dick is *aching*. I think for a moment I don't like her at all. I think I really will have to lock myself in the bogs for a while if we're going to be trailing round shops all afternoon. She has her wedgies on and her mouth is level with my ear when I hug her. I'm standing with my arse well back. May puts her hand on it and pulls me to her. My ma and da and all's away into Belfast to see my Auntie Ginny, she whispers. They'll not be back till late tonight.

*

West Berlin, November 1973

The first, wet snow of the year blows west along the Ku'damm, emptying the pavement of shoppers. The streets already have an odd, un-Saturday feel, as though no one can quite raise themselves to the weekend. There is talk now of a ban on Sunday driving, starting a week tomorrow; the energy crisis's invisible siege tightens.

Last Saturday, just here, on the corner of Fasanenstrasse, four students handcuffed themselves to the doors of a Mercedes. In their free hands they held megaphones through which they began denouncing the Egyptians for treating with Israel, then, after a while, they fell to shouting about Vietnam. The anti-American slogans had a comfortable ring to them, like jingles, or snatches of a favourite song. Passers-by looked at the four incuriously. Even the police did not appear to be in any hurry to remove them, for I could still hear their megaphone-shouts long after I had lost sight of them in the crowds. In the evening, I met a friend who had also seen the students, a little after I did, presumably. She said she had stopped on the opposite pavement to look across when suddenly a second car appeared alongside the Mercedes and a young man and woman jumped out. The woman wore a silver-grey fur coat and the man carried a camera. He followed her around the Mercedes taking pictures. She lay back across the hood, hung on to the shoulders of one of the students, snatched the megaphone from another, who being handcuffed was powerless to stop her. She posed once more with her hand on her hip, coat pulled back on a lime green trouser suit, and the megaphone at her mouth as though she was railing at the heavens, then she and the man jumped back in the car and drove away just as the police arrived from the opposite direction.

People applauded, my friend said. Only the bewilderment on the students' faces betrayed the fact that this was not all part of their happening.

Last Saturday it was pleasant enough to walk without a scarf and gloves. This Saturday the snow clings wetly to my face and hair.

I decide to take the U-Bahn to Gleisdreieck and walk to Willi's from there. As I am going down the steps at Uhlandstrasse, two women pass me going up, talking. I hear one of them say *fire* and I try, without success, to catch where it is she means, to see is it my fire they are talking about, the one I saw this morning.

It was early, six, six-thirty, I have not been sleeping well lately: pains in my leg. I had got up and gone for a walk. (Because, don't ask me why, the pain is easier if I am moving around.) There was already some traffic on the roads, people travelling to work, others perhaps only getting home. I had crossed the canal towards Schöneberg – it was in my head to walk as far as the Sportpalast, to see it one more time before the whole thing is pulled down – when I first noticed it, a building, an empty warehouse, in flames on a disused railway siding. The smoke alone was prodigious, an enormous black quiff curling from the top storey; a fringe of flame ran all around the eaves and there was fire too lower down, leaping in the window sockets. I walked closer. There was no one else to be seen, though cars were passing well within sight of the flames. It occurred to me, you notice these fires – sometimes, it seems, every day – and you listen to the radio, or you scan the newspapers, and there is no mention of them, as though what you had witnessed was as unremarkable, as inevitable, as human death.

I watched for ten minutes this morning as the warehouse burned. Still the fire brigade did not arrive. I wondered had anyone telephoned them, for even at that early hour, with so much smoke, someone else must have spotted the fire. Then I wondered at myself that I did not raise the alarm, and yet out there on the waste-ground, standing alone, the warehouse's burning appeared somehow natural, an act, almost, of volition. Stoical as a Buddhist monk, it blazed. I left only when I heard the sirens detach themselves from the other city sounds and draw near.

Afterwards, though, arriving back at the apartment, I felt a terrible emptiness. Guilt too. I could not believe that I had not checked to see was anyone inside the warehouse. I switched on the radio and waited for the news and of course there was nothing whatever about the fire. Even so, *I hadn't tried to check.* I left the apartment again, thinking to shop to take my mind off it, but it was no use. I needed to confide in someone, I needed to see Willi. Something has gone wrong.

But I feel it as soon as I board the train for Gleisdreieck that Willi is not going to be there. I come out of the station, turn off the street with the scrap-dealers (who do they sell to, when there is so much scrap, unless to each other?) and count my steps to the door of the *Kneipe*, trying in this way not to anticipate too much and raise my hopes. Even so, when I step inside and look around and do not see him, I am disappointed. The place is as good as empty, the light from the lamps more than usually dim. One of Willi's boys, one I have not seen before, has been left in charge. I ask where Willi is. The boy answers, as Willi's boys often do, in bad German, that he doesn't know.

Vous êtes français? I ask. His face brightens. *Oui, de Lyon. Et vous?*

I tell him I am not French. I tell him my lover was French but he died. *D'une surdose d'héroïne.* I don't know why I tell him this. He nods anyway. He is older than most of Willi's boys. Older but no less pretty for that. I wonder, as I often wonder looking at these young men, these refugees, what it is that Willi has that draws them to him. It cannot only be the offer of a roof; there are plenty of squats in Berlin, plenty of people willing to share their food with you, and without making you work as hard for it as Willi does. Likewise, there are plenty of people with Willi's contacts – and more – though it is true Fassbinder loves to come here when he is in Berlin, and Fassbinder has been known to meet a person one night and, just like that, the next morning to be standing them in front of his camera. But I tell myself such thoughts are unfair, Willi might not be much to look at, but he is kind and fun to be with.

For a time, when I first met him, he was married to an actor who in those days appeared often in plays and revues around the city. There was a woman – an eminent doctor and a collector of art – who had a flat in Charlottenburg, on the top two floors of the house she shared with her estranged husband, and on Saturday evenings people would gather there to talk about art and politics and listen to jazz. I was taken there shortly after I arrived in Berlin, by Konrad, who was then completing his studies, and who had some connection to the woman through her son. There were artists and writers standing on the balconies, drinking white wine, arguing points with their hands in the air; men and women – other doctors, lawyers, academics – dressed in polo-necks and open-necked shirts, sat in groups, or lay across the bed, debating. At one point I found myself standing alone, a little self-conscious. I felt a hand on my arm and looking up saw Willi:

Do you know, he asked me, the definition of chintz? *A material used by middle-aged couples to cover up the fact that they too were drunk when they met.*

Do you like that? he said. An English friend told it to me.

I said something, I don't remember what, in English.

But, my friend, Willi said, also in English, and his smile broadened still further. How wonderful.

And that was that. When Willi said my friend he meant it. Even after Konrad had left Berlin I continued to go along to the Frau Doktor's flat on Saturday nights, at first with Willi and his actor husband and then, when they parted, with Willi alone. Occasionally we would arrive to find an American soldier in one of the rooms with the other guests crowded around asking questions, about the war in Vietnam, about the youth protests. The soldiers who came of course were sympathetic. Many of them were homosexual, others, perhaps, simply curious. I was not shy, after that first night, even though I was only a student. I talked to politicians and famous names from television exactly as I talked to the men and women who sometimes came along who worked in factories and car-repair shops. I started an affair with an American soldier, one of those who was curious rather than queer, but that is another story.

I loved Berlin, for its vitality and its incompleteness. There was such a desire to *make use*, to build from this jumble something altogether new. Everything was experiment. The films too, they were a part of that: How far could you go? How far suppress the ego; efface yourself; infringe the boundaries of taste, knowing that those boundaries could encompass the burning of children?

Look at our bodies, look at these acts, these copulations. Look hard, do not turn away, this is nothing to be squeamish about.

They were energetic celebrations, *liberations*, to begin with.

It is hard to say when the first holes appeared and it started to feel as though something was leaking away. I have thought about this, and thought about this, and this is my conclusion: once the decision is taken to kill all your energy is consumed by that. There were too many people here at one time who decided to put their energy into destruction. Soon it becomes an end in itself. Wasting. Before long you are taking on the values that you claim to reject, your words become empty, your actions hollow.

I am almost twenty-six years old; I make pornographic films for a living.

I have a coffee and two cigarettes at Willi's. A man enters, drinks a beer standing up, and leaves. He looks my way as he goes out the door. A long look. He recognises me but does not believe it is me he sees. The boy at the counter reads a magazine. Every so often we glance at the clock at the same moment, catch each other's eye, smile a little awkwardly. It is hard to know how to sit and wait without looking as though you are sitting waiting. I try to remember exactly what I am waiting for, why it is so pressing that I speak to Willi, but my mind is suddenly blank.

I stand up and walk towards the door.

Salut, the boy says. *Salut*, I say back. *A bientôt*, though I know Willi with his boys: *plus jamais*, is more like it.

At the foot of the steps of the U-Bahn station a small man in an ankle-length overcoat proffers two packs of cigarettes, underhand. He does not seem to have any more about him, yet they are clearly for sale. He might have bought them from a shop and then changed his mind, or else have been given them by someone – a child or a lover – an unwanted gift. He holds them up a little higher as I approach and looks at me sceptically, almost defying me to buy them. I pass on, his hand drops, listless.

* *

"But what I still don't understand," Sam says, as though for the third or fourth time, "is why you kept your own name."

Ilse blinks down a sudden panic. There is no escaping anywhere. *He is even into her thoughts now.* But then, if he was, he would have read that one – would be reading *this* one. She holds her breath. Nothing but Sam's own expectant breathing. Perhaps, after all, she was not lost in thought, but actually talking out loud, and a new panic rises as she wonders for how long, in her exhaustion, she has been unable to distinguish between what is thought and what is spoken.

"I mean, most of the names you see in those films, they've got to be made up, right? So why not yours?"

Ilse has no real answer. It simply never occurred to her to change her name. (Though that of course, some might think, is answer enough.) At first, in fact, there were no names at all. Just people. *Friends.* She says as much into the darkness. She is aware of the compound absurdity of this conversation – for they are, clearly, she accepts, conversing by now, even if it is hard to shake off the suggestion of the confessional. Sam, unseen, prompts her, not against the impediment of her remorse, but of her utter detachment. Since Willi died she has not discussed this part of her life with anyone. She still has no idea how she came to be discussing it now.

"I was not ashamed of what I was doing then," she says. "It was a very particular moment."

Sam mentions a certain cinema off boulevard de Clichy. It might have felt like a particular moment, but all these years later the films are still out there.

"*Anyone* can walk in off the street and see you."

"It would not be me they were seeing," Ilse says.

"Aw, come on," he says (and his voice then, there is something familiar to her in the whine of it). "Come on, Ilse. I recognised you at once."

Ilse is silent a moment. It crosses her mind that Judgement Day, as her mother used to tell it, was to be like this, every last and least action called to account. (Though Judgement Day, if anything, might be less rigorous than a grilling by Sam with his obsession with detail and his need to know everything *NOW*.) She sees herself caught in the cone of the mountain, as though under the gaze of a celestial microscopist. She is aware once more that these might indeed be her last hours; but it is a distant awareness, for her last hours began so long ago it is getting harder by the moment to remember that there was ever anything else.

"When I was making the films" (and as she says this so it comes to life: there is the odd little man she was introduced to one fine day, with his serious, almost baffled expression and instant recovery after ejaculation – tick, tick, tick, My God! up it goes again; and there she is, barely able to move, she aches so much, but laughing, because – the look on his face! – this *is* funny) "I was able to live in a very fashionable address in Berlin. The apartments, you know, were quite grand. My neighbours were business people. If anyone had asked me what it was I did I would have told them, but no one asked. It was very discreet.

"This apartment, the bathroom, when I first went to look at it, was completely walled with mirror tiles. The person showing me round was a little embarrassed, I think. He had not lived there long enough, he said, to remove the tiles. But I fell in love with them straight away. It was not that I wanted always to be looking at myself. I did, I suppose, in a way, but what I liked was the . . . " She searches for the word: "multiplying." Then changes her mind, "No, *dividing* – you understand: more, more, more, but also less, less, less."

She pauses, letting her words catch up with her. She considers them. They will have to do.

"One day I arrived at a house where we were to make a film. I could tell the second I walked in the door, the way people were staring, that something was not right. And it occurred to me, once, on a day like this, everyone would have been my friend, and now scarcely a single person there knew me. There was a man on the first landing grooming a powerful Dobermann. He stopped as I approached. He and the dog both looked up. I turned about and walked down the stairs and into the street. I tried to smoke a cigarette, but I was shaking too much. I was angry with myself that I had not seen it coming. Not the business with the dog, the whole thing. It was a culmination. Everything had got turned around. I went back to the flat eventually and sat on the rug in my mirrored bathroom. And then . . . something happened, I had a nail-file in my hand and I was scraping the line of cement from around one of the tiles. It took me a long time. I had a hammer in the apartment – I had a whole bag of tools – but I did not want to break the tile, or even to crack it. I scraped and scraped with the point of the file till at last I had made a space to slip the blade underneath. The sound of the tile coming away from the wall was as sudden as a gunshot. I looked at the hole I had made, just below my left shoulder and saw it instantly transmitted – *ricocheting* – right around the room.

"It was easy after that. I worked – like a prisoner with my little file – all through the night taking the tiles down one by one, until only my eyes remained in a square above the wash-hand basin. I looked into them and I made myself say my name and then I prised them from the wall and the room went blank."

Beyond the mountain the generators hum.

"And that was it? You got out of it altogether then, the acting?"

The words come prefaced with a polite cough, almost as if

to apologise for having overheard. Their accent throws her, as does their unexpected trajectory. Yet in the next instant it strikes her as entirely appropriate that Raymond should join in in this way.

"I never wanted to be Jane Fonda," she says, more tartly than she intended; there was more than a little courtesy in his question (and more than courtesy, an acceptance). "I made some films, that was all. When they stopped making sense I stopped making them, as simple as that."

And in truth it was almost that simple. Only this complicated it:

Dean Bean (he looked you straight in the eye when he said his name) had for some weeks past been talking to cinema-club owners in his home town of New York, testing the waters and finding them very inviting to top-class product such as he was offering. Dean Bean glimpsed a future in these conversations and was far from displeased by it. He and Ilse Klein had been lovers since the late evening of the day they met, seven years before, at a party in a house in Charlottenburg. He had been a soldier then, a volunteer, rather than a draftee, but just as disaffected with army life as he had been with life at home working shifts, until he met Ilse. When at last his term of service was up he made his way back to Berlin. He worked for an American company advising on franchises to US army bases. His was a nothing job, a glorified messenger, but it suited his needs. He used his access to deal a little weed and, after a while, to organise film shows. It built up over time. Dean Bean wasn't suffering. Dean Bean was doing OK and aiming to do a whole lot better.

The day of Ilse's walk-out he called the house where the filming was to have taken place and was told what had happened. He got in his car and drove straight to Ilse's apartment and asked her what she was doing. She told him right out, *Nothing more*. Aw, come on, he said. Ilse, *Baby*, God's name, *Ilse*. He watched her watching him, unwavering. Then he hit her across the face. They were standing together in the bathroom with the mirror tiles. He liked to make love to her there, in the shower, on the rug. He hit her and in the turbulence of the air, in the undertow of the upsweep of his hand, she smelt money and fear from him, or more precisely, the fear born of money – which is the fear of loss. Her blood dripped from all her split lips, before her and behind her, to her left and to her right. He backed off. OK, he said. *OK, Ilse?* She nodded. He said, I'll come round for you tomorrow.

OK?

She nodded.

When he had gone she reached behind the sink for the little quilted bag where she kept her nail-file. She left the tiles in neat piles for him in the centre of the bathroom floor. Let him put them back again if he wanted.

He came into Willi's the next afternoon, knocking chairs over, demanding to know where Ilse was, threatening to scar her face for life. The customers, a lot of them, drew back into the corners. You could see it in his eyes, this American guy was out of control. Willi managed to quiet him a little. Ilse wasn't there, he said, he hadn't seen her for days, in fact he had been about to go looking for her himself, she owed him money. Dean let himself be talked into a back room while Willi went to fetch them each a beer. He sat in a chair and took off his patchwork leather cap fingering his long loose hair. Willi returned. Dean accepted the beer from him, closing his eyes as he took a pull, and instantly Willi pounced, breaking the bottom off his own bottle and pushing the jagged end to within an inch of the younger man's face. He had Dean by the front of his shirt and was pressing one knee against his gut to stop him throwing him off. Dean Bean, though, had already decided against it. (Perhaps he had heard from Ilse the story of how, as a child of ten, Willi had survived the Battle of Berlin on his own. Perhaps he reckoned that anyone who had had to fight to eat, even as a child of ten, might have depths to him that were best left only guessed at.) Willi told him if he ever heard of him looking for Ilse again he would have his eyes out. He whispered a couple of names in Dean's ear to emphasise the point, boys he had grown up with, gangsters now, whom he would telephone the instant this worthless piece of shit was off his premises.

Dean never did show his face again. Later that week, however, in the early hours of the morning, someone tried to set fire to the *Kneipe*, but they were either too incompetent or, when it came to it, too scared, for despite the discovery close by of a full can of gasoline the flames did no more than darken a corner of the doorway. Like the mark a sad old dog might leave, Willi said, lifting its leg. Some weeks later word got back to Ilse that her lover had left the city. It was some weeks after that, though, before she could bring herself to return to her apartment. The tiles of course had all been broken, ground underfoot, dumped in the shower and in the toilet. Blood stained some of the shards a reddy-brown. There were drips too, she noticed, retracing her steps, in the fibres of the carpet down to the doorway. One drop formed a perfect *Punkt* on the very threshold. Ilse drew the door closed over it and left.

There was a tiny museum, then just opened, off Nollendorfplatz, to the memory of the gay men and women persecuted by the Nazis. Two interconnecting rooms on the first floor of a house that had lost its attic to a wartime bomb. Very understated: photographs, playbills, letters, all leading to a case in which were folded two pairs of pyjamas, a pink triangle on one, a black triangle on the other. On the floor above, now the floor directly beneath the beams, was an even tinier café which Willi had an interest in. To begin with the staff had been volunteers, friends with a morning free, an hour or two to spare, but now that the spring was coming, bringing with it ever larger numbers of tourists, someone was needed to work it full-time. Ilse agreed to give it a try for a week or two. She stayed for fifteen years.

She moved into a smaller apartment in Wedding, almost on top of the Wall, her view into Prenzlauer Berg on the other side cut across distantly and at intervals by white and orange East Berlin trams, of which she never saw more than one car's length at a time, the exact width of the intersection. She was in love for a time with a painter who lived in the apartment below and once, after much persuasion, she consented to having her protrait painted against the backdrop of her window and the Wall beyond. (Ilse inclines her head towards the viewer as though trying to catch a comment or an instruction. There is a busyness about the foreground – in her face, in the coat cast carelessly over the arm of a chair, in the objects on the table: keys, coins, a theatre programme. The background, in contrast, is a study in inertia, save for the far left-hand corner where there is a blur of orange flank, like a fish glimpsed suddenly brilliant between the massed grey of rocks.)

She was in love at various other times with various other men, and even asked some to move into her apartment; a few stayed weeks, one or two, years, before, inevitably, she asked them too to move out again. These were her happiest years. She felt as though she had worked her way to the very edge of something, a phase in her life, or maybe just a line of thought, and found there, where she would least have expected it, a curious equilibrium. It seemed that all she had to do was wait. At moments she imagined herself pressed not against a wall, but a flawed mirror, in which the distortion revealed a truer reality than mere reflection ever could. She conjured up people on the other side, women like her, living similarly hopeful lives. Hopeful and expectant, because it seemed clear, here at the edge, neither East nor true West, that some mixture was possible, some other way. And then the Wall was less substantial even than a mirror: a membrane, rather, a bubble-skin.

But the rupture when it came caught her by surprise. (Though for many Monday nights past she had heard the tumult from Prenzlauer Berg's Gethsemane Church, she had not realised its import.) Where she had dreamt of exchange she witnessed only escape.

She hears her voice. She has been talking some of this to Sam and Raymond. She is telling them about the days after the Wall came down; how she finally persuaded herself to walk the short distance to Bornholmer Strasse and step over into the other side; how she stood at last at the junction across which, down the years, she had watched countless hundreds of trams pass, one car's length at a time, and turned her head to the left and to the right, like one released from a surgical collar. And – what did she expect? – it was grim. In either direction, block after block of featureless façades (except in so far as crumbling masonry could be said to be a feature) with here and there the symbol of the state-run Imbisses. She wondered at herself that she had thought this necessary to balance her own life.

Two elderly women, sisters perhaps, sharing a shopping bag, leaning out from each other, twisted like branches, shook their fists at her and shouted: *Go back! Go back! Leave us alone!*

She understood their shame. But of course there was no going back. Once the breach had been made, the Wall lost all its power to exclude. The gaps were patched haphazardly with wire fence and corrugated iron. Where once the forward march of fascism was to be halted, cats and dogs ran, children played with impunity.

No going back, but no going forward in the way Ilse had dreamt either.

The death-strip was transformed into property to speculate on (Daimler-Benz were first in, tying up Potsdamer Platz), the Wall itself into a commodity to be bought and sold, in lumps or in lengths. For a season there were no end of jokes and rumours about where it was being transplanted. It was wanted in Belfast, it was wanted in Paris, it was wanted, most of all, in Disney World. Nothing seemed so improbable it could not happen. It was as though the defining edge had been removed, wherever you looked you saw more of the same. The restored U-Bahn lines brought skinheads from the *Betonsilos* of the East, neo-Nazis who would congregate outside Zoo, their demeanours expressing equal parts cupidity and contempt, their hatred vented alike on wealthy Wessis and immigrants of all classes and ages.

Walking in Mitte very late one night, Willi was approached by a young man and invited to a party in a nearby *Hinterhof*. Somewhere along the way four more young men appeared and together with the first set about Willi with clubs and iron bars. He fought back like crazy – like Willi – but they were crazier by far. He did not die at once. Instead, he lay in hospital for many weeks, now going into decline, now showing signs of improvement, until finally he went into one decline too many and the electrical pulse which had been plotting the intricacies of his struggle evened out like a line drawn definitively under a life story. Ilse was there when the screens were switched off. Outside she bought a newspaper. She stared at the same page the length of the train ride home. It was only when she reached the apartment that her eyes cleared enough for her to read. Disney was coming to Europe.

Coming? she asked herself. Only now?

All the same, the next day she told them at the café she would soon be leaving and the day after that she withdrew her savings and bought a car.

* *

It was while Ilse was speaking that Raymond finally accepted as absolute the truth of what Sam had been saying all along about pattern. There are broad shapes here, even individual incidents, which evoke moments of his own life. There is correspondence, though it is shifting, one minute sitting up as sudden and exposed as a rabbit, startled, the next running chicanes through the obscuring undergrowth of local colour. But despite the shifts the momentum is relentless. Time and time again he is pitched helplessly into memory.

A Wednesday night in the monastery at Crécy-la-Chapelle. There is a match live on Sky Sport, European Championship; England need a point off Poland to go through to the finals in Stockholm; the Republic of Ireland have to win in Turkey and hope that England lose. The room to a man is up for the Irish. The Republic win 3 – 1. England trail for three-quarters of the game then pinch an equaliser ten minutes from time. Nobody in the television lounge says a word, but the frustration is written all over their faces. England always do it. The sense of injustice seems to fill the room; it is a collective sentiment, yet each man appears to feel it intensely individually. They look at the TV but seem from their expressions to have travelled elsewhere, revisiting some very personal location, the site, perhaps, of their first shameful recognition of the shadow they lived in. In this

they are all –Protestant and Catholic, unionist and national-
ist, don't-know and never-cared (for there are some) – Irish
together.

The adverts come on. The room becomes a chaos of
abandoned chairs. Men are moving towards the door when
the music starts up with a throaty surge, instantly silencing
their morose conversations. Raymond recognises the song
from first time around, "Twentieth Century Boy". On the
screen, ad-speed, a story unfolds, ad-logically. A handsome
youth is being released from a Southern American desert
jail. The guard, a silent-movie sadist, is furious at having to
let him go and refuses to give him back his clothes. But as he
leers at the youth standing, trouserless, in the desert sun, a
big convertible pulls up and a young woman throws the
youth a paper parcel. He undoes the string. Jeans. *Levis*.
Next she throws him a camera. She gets out of the car
wearing a short sequined sheath dress in which she proceeds
to strike exaggerated poses – all legs and shoulders – while
the youth takes pictures. The expression on the guard's face
sours behind the prison bars. The beautiful young woman
and the handsome young man, wheeling and snapping.
They get into the big convertible. As they drive off together
the boy tosses the camera towards the jail.

There is a moment in the television lounge – a pulse of
frustrated movement – as twenty-five pairs of hands resist
the urge to reach out and catch the camera. Men in track-
suits and slippers, sweat-shirts they got from filling station
promos, T-shirts that say G**nness Makes You Fart; men in
satiny football shorts and Argyll socks; men in sagging
Littlewoods denims. A concentrated stillness grips as the
camera lands in the jailer's hand, stretching from the prison
bars. Many heads dip into an unconscious nod. A mournful-
looking little man, a father of four from Tandragee,
whimpers.

That was the start of it.

All day Thursday, wherever you turned, there were stories about men (usually men who had recently jacked their jobs and gone home) having got off with women in Meaux, or even with one of the American women up on site. The entire enterprise was transformed, overnight, into an opportunity for licence. There was *sex* all around them.

The talk continued that night in the bar. Crazily, for there were still two days of the week left to work, many of the men seemed intent on getting completely obliterated. The tales now were of other contracts they had worked on, tales of their own sexual exploits, from Saudi and Iraq; of Asian servants, for that's what they were, who for a handful of dinar would do something more than clean your room for you; of leave time taken in Bangkok, and the twenty thousand reasons why no city ever deserved its name more. The bar throbbed with voices competing.

On Friday it was suggested they all go up to Paris the following night. Some of the younger men had already been, the single ones; they knew all the places to go. A few of the older married men said they were game; the rest wavered, and one by one throughout the day said they would go too. By dinner, the pressure on those who held out was intense.

"Sure for fuck sake, how's the wife going to know?"

"Imagine, a wee tight French fanny."

"Many weeks have you been here?"

"He's scared!"

"He's impotent!"

"No dick!"

"Some wee apprentice is creeping into his room at night!"

Raymond knew it did not pay to draw attention to yourself by not joining in, yet in this he was powerless. He simply could not go along. One night when he was on remand in the Crumlin Road, he heard his cell-mate moan and mumble in his sleep and looking over the side of the bunk saw a glistening wet patch spread from the lean pole butting at the waist of the other man's pyjamas. The sight filled him with something close to despair. Sex seemed so ignoble after that, stripped of meaning, a brute muscle's helpless thrashing. It could be someone you loved, it could be someone else altogether – someone you had only just met – whose name you did not even know; it could be no one but you and your cell-mate above you on a spring night when the great and the good and the not yet caught were still about their business in their houses and on the streets of Belfast.

The revellers returned at nine o'clock on Sunday night. Raymond was in the televison lounge with Simple Sandy from Belcoo, watching truck-driving from Kentucky or somewhere. Four or five of the men came to stand in the doorway. They pushed each other and giggled. Someone said something in an undertone and the rest collapsed in fits. They passed a duty-free bottle of Jameson's between them. Their faces were swollen red and voluptuous. At length one of them addressed the stay-at-homes.

"So what have we missed? Had yous anything nice for your dinner?"

Sandy, who perhaps after all was not as simple as he appeared, let on he didn't hear and kept watching the telly. Raymond, between him and them, turned and said:

"Rice and ravioli."

One guy (Raymond remembered him from Wednesday night, whimpering at the television), who had looked till that moment almost comatose, started up.

"They gave you rice?" he asked.

Raymond nodded.

"Fucking *rice*?"

Raymond nodded.

"For fucking Sunday dinner?"

The man pulled himself up indignantly and took a belt of the whiskey.

"I wouldn't even shit on it."

His companions cheered and slapped his back.

"Wouldn't even *shit* on it."

Raymond woke later, startled, in the chill darkness. Far below someone was shouting. *Fucking rice, for fucking Sunday dinner?* He looked at the clock beside his bed: twelve-fifty. The whiskey had not yet run out. Shoeless feet tramped past his door.

"Tommy says she just turned round and slapped the Vaseline up her arse and he went straight into her. Flipping wild, boy. Tell you another place too is wild for prostitutes, Tommy says: Rome. You'd think they'd be dead religious, know with the Pope and all there, but they're not a bit, they're dirty bastards."

Geese creaked in the yard. More feet passed Raymond's door.

"Did she take you into a wee room? Did you do it on a bed? Was it a wee hard French bed?"

Raymond cowled the pillow over his ears. His penis was a painful rod he almost wept to touch.

Perhaps it was on the way up to Paris that the men from the monastery finally got round to discussing him, piecing things together, this one talking to that one, that one remembering something this other one had told him.

There were Meaux men on the trip, and there were men from Meaux whom Raymond had recognised from having been inside. He thought a few times he had caught them looking at him, Protestants and Catholics. He had seen their hasty bipartite conferences. He knew it would not be long before they made the precise connection with his name. It was odd, there had been any God's number of scraps between loyalists and republicans since he arrived (Raymond had seen knuckle-dusters and knives – one night guns – produced), but there was too, on occasion, a kind of camaraderie, even respect. They were soldiers, was all, fated to fight, when fighting was called for, on opposite sides. And nobody respected a man who had deserted a comrade under fire.

Raymond had hoped by moving digs to take the pressure off. Men came and went all the time, once out of sight in the vulnerable night he would, with luck, quickly be out of mind. He hoped he would be able to see out the weeks to Christmas at the monastery without further examination.

He hoped in vain.

Your deeds, Raymond thinks, and thinks of Ilse, go out into the world like films. Once they are gone you have no control over them. Though you age and change, somewhere you exist as you were then, endlessly re-enacting the moment. So Ollie Thompson has been scripted into the epic tale of Ulster loyalism, a hero's part, revived every time the band that bears his name marches.

Raymond is in there somewhere too. He is Desertion. The man who abandoned a comrade. He is the surrender no one, but no one, wants any part of.

Raymond thinks of his wife and daughter. He wonders has anyone tried to contact them. He thinks life is beyond comprehension, that he should face the end of his in an unfinished mountain in the middle of France.

He is suddenly aware how long it has been since he was this close to anyone. He thinks, though, this is OK. In a way nothing really matters any more. He has been living all these years in fear of being discovered, hiding from who he is. But who he is is all right here too. Who he is is part of what this is about. The more reason there is for these things to be happening the easier they are to bear. He wants to add to the sum of Sam's and Ilse's understanding, as well as his own. He wants to tell them all he knows.

*

I was in the snooker hall this night with two friends of mine, Ollie Thompson and this fella called Gillespie. It was no particular night, I mean no night that wasn't like five hundred other nights we'd spent there from we left school. I was married – to May – six months and she was already expecting. We'd a house just down from my mother and father's. May didn't like me going to the hall when I could have been at home with her, but it would have suffocated you in that house, we were too young to be married at all. Some nights the three of us, Ollie, Gillespie and me, got a carry out – you know, tins of beer – and drank it in the back room of the hall, though by rights you weren't allowed. We'd talk about stuff, stuff that was going on, the same stuff we'd been talking about for as long as I could remember, bombings shootings the police the army the Provos the Prods. This night I'm talking about we'd some tins in and a bottle of vodka Gillespie had got somewhere or other, from some wee lads who'd asked him to go into the off licence for them probably. He was always doing that, taking their money and spending it himself. Him and I didn't get on the best, but Ollie was big mates with him, most of the time, and Ollie was my friend from I was no age, so the two of us just put up with each other.

I suppose we were drunk. I *know* we were drunk, but then we were drunk more than once in that back room, I'm not making any excuses, like I say, it was just a night like any other night, no better no worse. There'd been a solider shot earlier in Tyrone. (If I'd been to Tyrone once in my life that was all and that was once more than I'd have been to wherever it was the soldier came from.) A soldier shot and a bomb in town. We were in the snooker hall drinking the tins and Gillespie's vodka and Gillespie starts on about this fella Connolly from his work who's been shooting the mouth off.

"Connolly?" Ollie said. "Fucking cunt of a Fenian name if ever I heard one."

Gillespie, I used to think, liked getting people going, Ollie especially. Your man Connolly, he said, had been lifted one time by the army and held overnight at Girdwood barracks.

"Freddie says he seen him take his shirt off the other day and he'd *tiocfaidh ár lá* tattooed on his back."

"That's it, fucking definite," Ollie said.

He stood up and sort of fixed the waistband of his trousers and then he was holding a gun in his hand, panting a little, like a conjuror after his big trick.

"Aw, shite, Ollie," Gillespie said.

His eyes were shining.

"Aw, shite, nothing," Ollie said. "Come on ahead. Are you in or are you out?"

I was just sitting there looking at all this like it was completely separate from me. Ollie waving the gun around, asking Gillespie where your man lived. It was like . . . it didn't seem *unusual*. . . One minute the gun wasn't there, the next minute it was, like I always knew somehow it would be if we sat there long enough.

I was thinking as soon as they get up to leave I'll go on home to May.

Gillespie had stopped protesting. How are we going to get there? he asked and Ollie said, sarky, take a bus, what do you think? I'll tell you exactly what I think, Gillespie said, I think you'd better ask yourself who's going to drive us there if we don't. Ollie looked at him – none of the two of them could drive – then nodded at me. It'll have to be Raymond. *Raymond*, Gillespie said. Raymond can't drive. Aye he can, said Ollie. Can't you? I have my provisional, I said. Fucking great, Gillespie said, we'll steal a car with L-plates on.

Talking about it like that, killing someone, made it seem even more removed, just one thing after another to overcome. I was wondering would Ollie think it was worth the bother. But Ollie was all up for it. I suppose now he actually had the gun out of his trousers he wasn't going to put it back till he'd used it.

I'll be all right driving, I told Gillespie. It's not as if I'll have to be reversing round corners or anything.

I don't know what made me say it. I think maybe I just wanted to get it over with and go home to May. I was telling myself half an hour and that'll be it, Ollie can do what he wants in future. I felt perfectly sober, absolutely stone cold.

Gilliespie said what about masks. Good thinking, Ollie said. That was them friends again. They were always getting on like that those two. Ollie started going on about balaclavas and how they made it more professional, same way you never saw the faces of the firing squad before they shot you, they were just guns without personalities.

Do you remember, Gillespie said, when you were a wee lad, the flipping helmets you had to wear? (When we were wee lads we were all out in a permanent rash from October to March from the scratchy wool of our helmets.)

Do you still have yours? Ollie asked him. I think he was joking.

Gillespie went off looking for money bags or something we could cut holes in, and Ollie and I went to get a car. We found one open, keys in it and everything, out the back of the snooker hall. I told Ollie we'd be better taking one from somebody's house, threatening them not to go to the police for three hours or whatever, but Ollie said this is a flipping gift, we'll have it back before the owner even knows it's gone. A Vauxhall Viva it was. Only two doors, which was a mistake, though it never occurred to me and Ollie.

(Ilse said: "Once in Stuttgart I stole a car with only *one* door. What they call in England a *bubble car*. I was very, very – you understand – young at the time. It belonged to a man, a lover. My first. He was married. He would not see me any more, so I stole his bubble. I drove it out of the city, singing a song I made up myself about what a useless lover he was. Then suddenly I had no more gas. In the middle of the mountains, twenty, thirty kilometres from home. The stars were all around my roof. It was beautiful. When the police found me I could not speak for crying. I was so happy."

Sam stirred between the two car thieves, filliped by this new unlooked-for proof.

"The two doors," he urged Raymond. "Go on.")

Gillespie was waiting for us where we said we'd meet him. I don't know what sort of bags they were he'd got in the end, but there were eye-holes already made in them. Sticking out, Ollie said. Gillespie got in the passenger seat to give me directions. Ollie was in the back with the gun. The idea was that they would swap over when we got to the house. I was concentrating on driving the car, all's I'd ever driven was an Allegro. Everything seemed to be in the wrong place. The engine cut out on me at the first set of traffic lights I hit, a couple of hundred yards down the road. Why don't we just stop at a phone and get the AA to tow us there? Gillespie said. Shut you up, I told him, I'm doing my best, aren't I? I felt like getting out then and there and walking away. The car behind tooted its horn. Ollie looked out the rear window. He's doing his best, he said. I pulled the choke out and tried to start it up again, pushing down hard on the accelerator. The car leapt forward just as the lights turned back to red. I swerved to avoid a car coming at me from the left, mounted the pavement on the right, came off it again, crossed the road and smashed into a minibus parked in the lay-by. Our whole passenger's side buckled. Gillespie pulled his legs away just in time. He rolled over against me. Get out the fuck! he shouted. The door on my side was bent too. I was hitting it and hitting it with my shoulder. There were sirens everywhere all of a sudden. I yelled at Ollie, I told you we should have taken another car, I told you. I was crying. Gillespie leaned across me and hit the driver's door a thump and it flew open. The two of us scrambled out and started running. Ollie was hunting on the floor for the lever to fold the front seat forward. He still had the gun in his hand. Chuck that thing away! I shouted at him. He shouted something back I didn't catch. A helicopter appeared from somewhere, flying low, flinging its searchlight about like a big net. The place was already swarming with cops yelling at everybody to freeze. (they really do say freeze) and again Ollie shouted out behind me – I was nearly sure this time it was fuck he was shouting –and then all I heard was the guns going off.

You can tell the instant somebody's died, you know. It's as though there's one less sound in the world when the shooting ends than there was before it started. I stopped running and let the helicopter beam catch up with me. I stood there in its circle of light with my hands in the air, thinking that's it all over. I'm twenty-one, married six months to a woman who's four months' pregnant. I told myself this was what it was going to be like from now on. I couldn't see how I was ever going to step out of that circle. Gillespie was standing with his hands up on the opposite footpath from me. It felt like there was more than just a road between us.

*

While Raymond was inside, May gave birth to a baby girl, Stephanie Rosalind, whom he saw for half an hour twice a week while on remand, and thereafter half an hour one week in every two. The baby was six months old before he saw her awake at all. She opened her eyes one afternoon and looked at him incuriously, pulling in her half-inch kink of bottom lip, then looked at her hands closed around the satin border of her blanket.

While Raymond was inside, a new band was formed round where he lived, the Ollie Thompson Memorial Flute Band. A mural was painted on the side of the Mace (which not only offered the largest wall locally but had the added advantage of being visible to residents of a nearby Catholic estate): Ollie, from an old passport photo, nestling in flags. Ollie.

At primary school he had been teased by the older boys about his name. Another fine mess. And now they had named a flute band after him, and painted up a mural. In proud and loving memory. His name, restored to its full birth-certificate complement of six letters, was raised in the House of Commons where a Unionist MP tabled a question about police tactics. Ollie had died with one foot caught under the front seat of the car. That was what he had been shouting to Raymond. I'm stuck.

When *he* was on remand, Gillespie was born again. The Holy Spirit moved him to repent of all his sins. The trial judge accepted that he had acted under duress and reduced his sentence accordingly.

By the time Raymond was released, the wall with the photo-booth mural had been demolished. Car-parking space for a new DIY superstore. The authorities were just starting then in earnest to clear the old battle zones, but, if anything, the landscaped divisions seemed to Raymond more difficult to overcome than what had gone before. Houses were no longer built in streets, but in closes, inward-looking.

The Ollie Thompson Memorial Flute Band were out that

spring collecting door to brass-knockered door for new uniforms for the marching season ahead. Raymond passed up the invitation to contribute.

It struck him as curious that while the city was attempting a more benign aspect, its parades had become more blood-curdling and overt. Civil servants and bank employees, church committee members, rotarians, urbane after-dinner speakers, marching to the beat of a drum on whose blood-speckled skin was the name of a youth who had set out to take a life. And then there were the people who lined the routes of the parades, with their newfangled camcorders and their fold-away chairs, the people who did not switch off their camcorders or fold away their chairs when the Ollie Thompson Memorial Flute Band passed by; or any of the other bands with their paramilitary colour parties, their flags of homage to this Volunteer, or that Commando, Ulster's extinguished Freedom Fighters. But the spectators of course, like the marchers, were safely encased in pageant, just as Ollie Thompson, dead at twenty-one, was encased in the pageant of the past. Perhaps the circumstances of Ollie's death had obscured what he was actually about when he died. Raymond was an unwelcome reminder of that. *He* had lived. *He* remembered what it was like in the Viva that night, the chemical-pine and beer smell of murder become rote.

*

"Gillespie was an informer," Sam says.

"I know," Raymond says.

"So why did you never tell anyone?"

"Because if he hadn't been I would have been a murderer."

Talking, Raymond and Ilse find, warms them, or at least makes them forget for the present how cold they are. (And make no mistake they are cold, their skulls, tightened, ache with the effort of sequential thought.) And talking, too, diverts their minds from the time and time is the one thing neither of them wants to dwell on, for time in the mountain is without rhythm and thwart: thirty minutes can pass in what seems instants, and a handful of seconds can weigh like hours. The cavern all the while expands and contracts with the sweep of the lights; it is a hidey-hole and a universe, the be all and end all and a near nothing. But shrunken or inflated, what lies beyond it in space as in time is plain surmise. Here and now is where they are and they must get through each distorted moment as best they can. So they talk.

Ilse contributes a story she read in a newspaper the last time she visited Stuttgart. A group of art students had travelled from the city to the country – it was the end of the school year – and, with official blessing, had erected an eight-metre high papier-mâché model of the Venus de Milo in a clearing in a wood. The pastor of the church in a nearby village had protested against its installation, its *nudity*, and one night, his protests having gone unheard, he led a number of his congregation to the woods and together they removed the offending breasts and buttocks *with a chainsaw*.

Raymond adds the tale of a man he knew who lost his wife, and his house, in a fire and bought a million and one things with the insurance money trying to start again: a Parker-Knoll chair, a three-piece suite in genuine leather, a bathroom suite in white and gold, two good beds for the two guest bedrooms, a Persian rug for the hall, an Afghan rug for the lounge, a picture for every wall, mirrors, plants, clocks galore, a 26″ colour television, a Betamax video-recorder, the first of its kind, a VHS when Betamax's fortunes went into decline, a set of Waterford crystal glasses, six for red wine, six for white, six for whiskey, bottles of whiskey, bottles of wine, stacks of books from stacks of book clubs, a stack-system hi-fi, every Ronco record, every K-tel compilation, ever advertised, a Bontempi organ, a tuba on which he never got further than oom-pah-pah oom-pah-pah, a whoopee cushion, just for a laugh, a dog to walk, a cat to stroke, dog and cat baskets, stuffed-snake draught excluders, gonks, ornaments, whatever caught his eye in Sunday colour supplements – collectables and disposables, jewellery and frippery – a week-by-week encyclopaedia of cookery, a month-by-month encyclopaedia of everything else, a new tool for his toolkit every fortnight, a wooden block containing The World's Sharpest Knives, by means of one of which, when his life still refused to add up, he cut his throat, reclining on the Parker-Knoll chair, while clocks galore struck twelve (his feet, convulsing brought one crashing down to stop, short, on the Afghan rug). He left a note. Sorry, it said, I tried everything.

Sam is happy to let them talk. Every syllable binds them to him more completely, their memories, their lives, becoming by degrees one with his own. Their stories in a sense are not so much revelations as reminders, for he feels now he has been in covert communion with these people all along. He sees them abroad through the years of his growing, gathering information, silent and assiduous; sleepers he has activated. They have acquitted themselves well. He reviews, again, his own road to their rendezvous and is satisfied that even when the ground seemed shifting sand beneath his feet his progress was unerring.

0330

Sous les pavés, la . . . The graffito faded into the shadows from the imploded doorway of a house, fallen into dereliction, in the crook of the dog-legged rue des Boulangers. A less cryptic communiqué had been stencilled in red on the exterior brickwork: *Interdiction d'entrée à Mathieu.*

Sam was reading walls, trying to find his way. It was the first weekend after his arrival in France and he had come up to Paris with his house-mate, Kent Weinberger, for a day's sightseeing. Kent was waiting for him right about now by the Fontaine de Médicis in the Luxembourg gardens where the two had parted earlier that afternoon. Sam looked up rue des Boulangers in his city guide, walked a step, tilted the map a little to one side, and started back the way he had come.

He didn't know where the afternoon had gone. He had remained in the gardens for a time after leaving Kent, stopping in the shade of the poplar trees to watch the groups of men playing their peculiar Tarot-trumps; he had strolled, purposefully, the boulevards around the Sorbonne, but very soon, and without his intending it, the trail of his logic had gone cold and he found himself following the bidding of the streets, across the river and back again, until he arrived, at three minutes after four in the dog leg of the rue des Boulangers.

As he exited the street he paused to place it and its surrounds in his memory. The connection once made would stick. He loved the way the complex circuitry of cities yielded to the patient eye their eventual reason.

Don't see the problem, look for the solution.

Disney training. Sayings such as this – posted on bulletin boards, framed above work stations – were among the first things you noticed on arrival at Walt Disney Imagineering back in Glendale, California. The morning of his own arrival the sun was a perfect tight circle, balanced like a beacon (if he closed one eye) on the pinnacle of the flagpole which rose almost as high as the two-storey building itself. Little else distinguished the façade from the industrial units which surrounded it on Glendale's Flower Street. The lack of ostentation struck Sam as entirely appropriate. This was a job, after all, same as any other. He was met in the lobby by a guy, not much older than he was, who gripped his wrist when they shook hands and introduced himself, a fraction of a second after his name tag did, as Marlon. Surnames were surplus to requirement at Walt Disney Imagineering. Sam was given a tag of his own, then and there: three red letters and the Mouse's smiling face. Marlon led the way, past aerial photographs of the parks at Anaheim, Orlando and Tokyo, to the cafeteria – the Big D Disney Dream Diner – where he ordered them both – milk? Sam gestured, *sure* – and cookies. There was a buzz in the room, serious but excited. People *enjoyed* their work here. Marlon caught the drift of Sam's thoughts.

"You know," he said, "there are days when I wake up and think I must be the luckiest person alive."

Sam nodded. Over Marlon's shoulder he could see a life-size figure of Walt himself. (Already the first name did not feel in the least over-familiar.) The face was amiable, to the point where Sam half expected one or other of the eyes to close at any moment in a wink. A young woman, wearing a red and white spotted bow in her hair, approached the table. Marlon rose part way out of his chair as she bent to hug him.

"Consuela," he said. "I want you to meet Sam."

Consuela took Sam's hand in hers and, just as Marlon had earlier, laid hold of his wrist as she shook it. It was, Sam understood, a handshake full of the promise of future friendly hugs.

"Consuela is one of the stars of Research and Development," Marlon said and Consuela rolled her eyes.

"There are days," she said, sitting down, "when I wake up and think I must be the luckiest woman alive."

Marlon's head was bobbing in appreciation of her testimony.

"Absolutely," he said and Sam joined in, under his breath, "Absolutely."

As he was leaving the cafeteria with Marlon, Sam saw coming towards them a guy with the easy-going roll of a veteran high-school coach. Marlon tugged lightly on Sam's sleeve.

"*Splash Mountain*," he said, out the corner of his mouth.

"*Him?*" Sam whispered and Marlon nodded as the three drew level.

"One of them."

"Hey, Marlon," the guy said, and with the slightest of glances at Sam's cardigan, "Hey, Sam."

Such encounters, Sam soon learnt, were part of the daily round at Walt Disney Imagineering; one minute it was Mr Splash Mountain, the next Mrs Captain Eo, so that it was all Sam could do those first few days to keep from pinching himself. These people were *history*; these people, some of them, remembered Anaheim when it was no more than orange groves, had traded ideas with Walt about the construction of EPCOT, had stories to tell of the race to get Abraham Lincoln ready for the '64 New York World's Fair. ("The first day we set up in the Illinois Pavilion the President did everything exactly the way he had in trials in California, but then, just as we were beginning to congratulate ourselves, he went and threw a fit. And our hearts, you know, are in our mouths, but the guy sitting beside me, he didn't panic. Hell, Abe, he said, I know how you feel. New York gets me that way too.") These were people, Marlon said, could make a rock speak.

"If you can dream it, they can animate it."

There was another famous saying Sam first heard about this time, one of Walt's: *Nothing has to die.*

And when you looked around you inside the unassuming shell of 1401 Flower Street, when you saw the quiet determination on the faces of the men and women in the Big D Disney Dream Diner, it was easy to believe it, nothing did have to.

Kent was waiting by the fountain reading *The European*, drinking a soda that had cost him, in all probability, way too much. Store bags at his feet charted his afternoon's journey. Kent's mother (like his serial fathers) was an executive in the movie business; professional mergers and personal separations had variously inflated her private wealth, and Kent's. His Imagineer's salary was pocket money to Kent; he could spend a month's in a day and not miss a penny of it in the morning.

"Hey, what's up?"

"Sorry," Sam said. "I lost track of the time."

Kent signalled with his hand that apologies were unnecessary. A woman was feeding bread to sparrows at a nearby hedge. The birds came up one at a time to sit on the rail before her pinched fingers, dipping their heads like communicants for the proffered bread.

"Man, did you know there's a *war* on here?" Kent said. "A proper war: air-raids and all kinds of shit."

He folded the newspaper to an inside page and handed it to Sam. A man, his face a rictus of full-coloured agony, was being borne towards a hospital bed by three distraught orderlies.

"They're wasting an entire *city*."

Frowns were foreign to Kent's face, and the frown which sat there now pressed down on his brow like it hurt.

Sam scanned the headlines beneath a red, white and blue flag ripped asunder. The names though – Croatia, Serbia, Vukovar – seemed in every way so distant it was difficult, even with the aid of photographs, for the mind to get a purchase. The sun, the breeze in the trees, the calm of the gardens made the story appear overstated.

Disconnected from the immediate stimulus of the newspaper, Kent's frown could sustain itself no longer.

"What do you say we go take a look at Notre-Dame?"

The cathedral was besieged by tourists, the square in front heaved with their ebb and flow. Children, separated from their parents, cried; parents, panicked, called and scolded. Sam suggested they leave the cathedral for another visit and go some place else. Kent thumbed through his guide book.

"Montmartre?" he said.

"All right," said Sam. "Montmartre."

It was three Métro changes from Hôtel de Ville to Pigalle and the two Americans surfaced on boulevard de Clichy into a late-summer evening just beginning to pink at the edges. They wasted no time abandoning the avenue and climbing the streets twisting up the side of the Butte Montmartre. The sidewalks and staggered passageways were quiet; an occasional turn would bring them of a sudden upon a small group composing itself for a photograph beneath a plaque, a couple kissing in the shade of a tree, children tumbling from a Citroën parked before an out-of-the-way restaurant. Nothing more. Where the people came from, then, who thronged the place du Tertre just below the Sacré-Coeur, the goal of their climb, was not immediately clear. They gave the impression of always having been there, poring over prints of the same streets, in which people, unlike themselves only in dress, sat, calm in their ascendancy over the softening city.

Still, the tourists here seemed of a different, less frenetic order to those who overpopulated the square before Notre-Dame. Kent opted to remain among them and take the benefit of the view, while Sam carried on up the steps to the church.

Within the doors of the Sacré-Coeur the outside light was muted to a brown heaviness. To the left, as Sam entered, a statue of the Virgin Mary was raised on a pedestal and around her feet were massed eight tiered tables bearing white candles, a few new-lit, others near guttering, most somewhere in between. Sam felt the awakening of a familiar awe (for the effect was as arresting in its artlessness as Main Street illuminated at night with its thousands of unadorned bulbs), which was transformed a moment later into something less certain by the realisation that each of these flames represented a prayer, the tables together a metropolis of thanksgiving and anguish.

A girl of seven or eight approached the statue with her father. She was a clumsy, homely-looking child, rendered still plainer by eye-glasses which appeared to have been fashioned for a much older face, and her front teeth bit bloodlessly into her bottom lip when she walked forward, as though the simple act of keeping upright and mobile

demanded her utmost concentration. She dropped a grace-
less curtsey to the Virgin and slotted a coin into the wooden
box at the statue's feet, selecting a candle in exchange. Her
father, at her shoulder all the while, found her a space on one
of the lower tiers and at his direction the girl lit the wick from
a neighbouring candle (prayer igniting prayer, so that it was
possible to imagine the flames never going out) and pressed
the butt down on to the holder's metal spike. She brought
her hands together and lowered her head a moment, then
raising it again looked to her father, who gave her the
approval of his smile. She returned her gaze to the candle,
burning with her prayer.

Sam took a step back, steadying himself against the rail of
a side chapel. The child was utterly transfigured by the
devotion. Her glasses were a hundred flames, her eyes, at the
centre, were lustrous black. *She was beautiful*.

Feeling suddenly at a loss, he joined the movement of
people along the left-hand aisle. Here and there a person sat
in unfathomable silence, eyes fixed, overtaken by adoration.
By one alcove, two elderly Japanese women, unseasonably
dressed in mackinaws, were examining the base of another
statue. They hesitated, conferring, before the bolder of them
reached out and picked up the objects lying there, turning
with them to two equally elderly Japanese men, stood just in
front of Sam. In one hand the woman held a strip of pills
from which two capsules had been taken, in the other hand
the capsules themselves, left beside the foil wrapper, as
though after all unnecessary. The Japanese crossed themselves and Sam, unthinking, felt his own thumb and
forefinger touch the bridge of his nose, his sternum and the
soft slopes of his breast.

Arriving again at the foot of the nave he lowered himself
into a rush chair, looking down the body of the church to the
sacré coeur itself, a bright light shining from the centre of

Christ's chest, throwing out rays to the kings and the saints sheltering beneath the canopy of his outstretched arms. Sam could not drag his eyes away. The impression, when you gazed hard, was almost three-dimensional. The rays were jets of gold, miraculous balm raining down. And then, at a certain moment, the image seemed to change, the jets of gold became as chains, the Christ's heart was in fetters and the prayers of the people were pulling it down. The Son of God stood in the great dome of the church with his hands widespread and said, *Take it*.

Sam stared until his eyes blurred, crying for the sacred heart torn out.

Kent found him some time later, slumped in apparent sleep. Sam leapt at the touch of his friend's fingertips on his shoulder. Kent leapt at the sight of Sam's face, streaked with his recent tears.

"Gee, I'm sorry," Kent said. "I didn't know. . . I mean . . ."

"No," Sam said. "It's OK. Really, it's OK."

His memories of the descent from the *mont* were scanty. The entire city now seemed enveloped in the church's reverent light. He walked, in near silence, with his housemate Kent, along Rochechouart and Magenta to the Gare de l'Est. The summer Sunday evening sidewalks overflowed with life. The people strolling, browsing through the stalls under the arch of the Barbès-Rochechouart Métro, had the studiedly unrehearsed air of participants in a ritual. On the train back to Meaux, Sam recalled having seen on one of the vestibule walls in Sacré-Coeur a plaque, dated 1919, declaring Paris a city of prayer, dedicated to Christ. He remembered too, earlier, his faith that he could find his way around its streets. No route was accidental, no movement, no turn, unforeseen.

They were leaving the city's eastern suburbs now. The

fences at the side of the track were dense with murals. An out-of-commission train, balanced on concrete blocks, had been transformed by graffiti artists into a strip cartoon. Carriage by carriage, in the time it took the Meaux train to pass by, it told the story of the youth of the district, who loved who, the music they listened to.

Sam turned from the window, fired with a sudden insight, but before he could give utterance to his thoughts his eyes were drawn away from Kent's face to the view from the window opposite. On an outcrop of wall a ten-foot high caricature of Mickey Mouse, delinquent in dress and demeanour, hunched, grimacing, over a giant syringe embedded in the crook of his arm. A scroll, curved like a halo around his head, bore the legend *fils de Mickey*.

Sam blinked the vision away.

Coincidence, he reassured himself, as the train rattled over a point and his whole body shuddered.

*

Coincidence.

Leaving Flower Street late one night, a fortnight before he was due to travel to France, Sam decided on the spur of the moment to drive towards Downtown for something to eat. He pulled in at a gas station along the way. An ancient VW Bug, caked in red dust, drew up on the opposite side of the pump. A woman in early middle age got out, barefoot, and opening the trunk bent over the engine. The floor and passenger seat, seen through the open door, were a mess of fast-food cartons and water bottles, an incense stick leaked smoke from a Buddha squatting in the ashtray. Something stirred in Sam, a memory that was closer in texture to a dream. The woman let down the hood and came back round to the driver's seat, leaning across to the glove box, feet still on the tar. *Her* feet, without doubt. It was the weirdest thing observing her this close up after so long, unreal this sensation of being dropped without warning into the film of somebody else's life.

And then at the very last moment, as the woman straightened in her seat and looked at him directly for the first time, aware of his scrutiny, Sam doubted that it was her at all, for he now noticed that she wore round her neck a silver chain from which was suspended an italicised silver name. Diane.

The woman regarded him narrowly for a second or two and then said, without surprise, *Hey, it's little Sam*.

"*Jen?*"

The woman smiled, fingering the chain at her throat.

"Then."

They drove together to a diner a little down the highway from the gas station. She had been on her way up the coast to Pismo Beach, to see an old friend, she told him, when on an impulse she had steered the Bug inland towards the desert.

"Coincidences," she said, "are pearls we collect and string together."

She was ten and a half now. She had abandoned the name Jen the same day she had abandoned Jennifer, the day she left New Dawnland for good and all. It had taken time, and several aborted flights, but after a certain point she had just ceased altogether to believe in the commune. Unlike Sam's parents, though, she had chosen to come back to the city, to the neighbourhood where she had grown up, in fact, in South Central. She got by for a time, the way she always got by, telling fortunes, until every future she foresaw looked the same and people round there, she realised, were losing interest in tomorrow. Nowadays she was working in a centre caring for children of jailed single parents. *Problem kids*, by their very existence, who would grow up (if they were lucky) into invisible adults, the people whom the Downtown developments and upscale housing projects, with their entry gates and sentries, were designed to guard against.

"Paradise costs a fortune in locks these days," Diane said.

She asked Sam about Holly and Tom. He told her about the studio-cum-gallery they had moved into the year before, by the harbour to catch the summer trade. Told her about the gallery, but made no mention of the security system they had spent all winter and thousands of dollars installing; even in Maine, they said, you couldn't be too careful.

She asked about Jennifer. Sam toyed with a napkin. Jennifer, uh, was – last he heard – reading horoscopes on a local cable channel. *Luck, Love, Money, and You.*

Diane chewed her last mouthful of bean-and-cheese, thirty-two times plus; swallowed.

"And what about you, Sam? What are you doing in LA?"

He had avoided saying anything too specific up to now. For as long as he could remember he had had to deal with the disapproval of his parents and their friends to his chosen Disney-life, but now he realised he had grown as comfortable fielding their objections as they had making them. Jen – Diane – though was an altogether more awkward proposition. Faced with her direct question, however, he had little option but to talk. He began, haltingly, watching for the inevitable smirk. But none came. She heard him out in respectful silence then leaned across the table and touched the whitened knuckles of his right hand.

"It's as good a place as any to make a difference," she told him.

Sam was to call her, but never did. A few days later he flew back to Maine for a week's vacation before carrying on to France. The connecting flight ran into a thunderstorm ten minutes out of Chicago and the plane had to put down at the airport again for a couple of hours. Sam settled himself for the lay-over, on his lap a copy of his umpteenth Disney biography, a trashy scissor-and-paste job (he could nearly have written one of these things himself by now) he had picked up, almost without thinking, from a rack in the terminal at LA. He had been working flat out getting ready to leave for France. He was exhausted. The words of the book swam on the page before his eyes. On the edge of his field of vision, the arrival and departure screens kept up a flickering electric blue rhythm, announcing new delays. A pair of middle-aged twins bickered before them, prodding one another's chests with matching tennis rackets; a child was sobbing out of sight, saying he wasn't getting back on the plane. Sam struggled to block out everything but the biography. He managed to re-focus for a minute or two more, then his head dipped and the words fled completely.

He was in a room furnished with three large leather chesterfields, around and between which ran a model railroad track. Hand-held games consoles lay on the cushions and floor, pinball tables were ranged the length of one entire wall; television sets switched, unaided and out of sync, from sports channels to old movies and back again on eight of the nine low tables which he counted dotted about the room. The ninth table, in a dimly lit corner, supported instead a spectacular cake encased in pink frosting. Two figures were bent over this table in heated conversation and though Sam could not make out their words he knew they were arguing about the correct number of candles to put on the cake. This was Jen's room, the 29 February room, the room of the extra day; and as if to lend credence to the thought, at that moment one of the televisions floated up and came to rest six feet above the surface of its table.

"She's eleven next birthday," Sam said.

At the sound of his voice, one of the stooped figures straightened.

"What do you say?"

His interrogator turned on him a disconcertingly round, flat face, frayed at the edges with age and stubble. He wore sweats of faded blue, ingrained with grime, and a pair of threadbare checkered house slippers. Thick-lensed eyeglasses dangled from a chain drooping to his tubby breasts. Only his hands interrupted the theme of dilapidation, covered as they were by neat-fitting white gloves.

"What do you say?"

Sam backed off.

"I was only trying to help."

"Sure," the round-faced man said. "Help."

Sam sat on one of the chesterfields. A train whistle sounded below him and he moved his feet apart just in time to let a steam locomotive pass between them.

"Watch it, bud," a voice said and Sam was sure he saw a tiny fist shake at him from the locomotive's cab; the whistle sounded again. "Final call for Washington, DC."

The round-faced man had put on the eye-glasses and was giving Sam a good looking over.

"What's the big idea anyway, sneaking in here?"

Sam started to explain about the thunderstorm, but the man cut him short with a wave of a white-gloved hand (which was missing a finger, Sam noticed).

"But we don't know you. – Do we?" he asked the figure still preoccupied with the cake behind him.

All he got in reply was a grunt, though he seemed to think that affirmation enough.

"Just showing up like that? We don't know who the hell you are."

Sam, irritated, the more he thought about it, that this man

should be giving *him* the third degree in his friend Jen's room, was moved to shout back.

"Yeah, well, I don't know who the hell you are either."

The man winced as though wounded, eye-glasses jerking on their chain as they slipped from his twitching nose. But the hurt expression that had begun to spread over his face was suddenly halted. He tugged at his ears, which stretched, as easily as chewed gum, till they were hanging limp along the curves of his jaw. His face meanwhile had darkened and become even flatter, his nose shrivelling to an inkspot beneath black tombstone eyes.

"Recognise me now?" he asked, trying to hold on to his breath.

Sam recognised him all right, couldn't imagine in fact how he had failed to recognise him before now, but his mouth, as if still disbelieving, could not give tongue to the name.

The man, *thing*, breathed out. His features resumed their former dimensions, though the imprint of the make-over seemed to linger about them, like a transparency.

"Oswald," he said, extending a hand.

Sam shook it. Three fingers, no mistake: "*The Lucky Rabbit*," he said.

Oswald gave a half-hearted laugh.

"Lucky? Not me."

He pointed to the floating television and instantly a younger version of his self-caricature careened around the screen in mute histrionics aboard a monochrome trolley-bus.

"There's the lucky guy," Oswald said. "I did all the spadework and the kid gets the glory. Luck?" He snapped his fingers. "I ain't never had that much luck in my whole life. Said I lacked – what was it? – *youthful appeal*; said I lacked", Sam almost beat him to it, "vigour. But age doesn't matter in this game" – he turned a pirouette of remarkable

grace, bowed, and fell backwards over a chesterfield —
"Timing's the thing."

He picked himself up, unhurt.

"You ought to have known me then: *Walt Disney Presents
OSWALD THE RABBIT in 'Poor Papa'*. You ever see it?"

Sam shook his head. Oswald's finger remained crooked in
the air, an expectant question mark which he quickly erased
with another wave of his hand.

"You young people, you know nothing."

(Poor Papa Oswald, Oswald the Unlucky Rabbit
Too fat and too old — too many damned kids —
To cut the cartoon mustard.
Poor Papa Oswald, the Daddy of them all —
The mice and ducks and dogs that made the Disney
billions —
Screen-tested and found wanting
Abandoned — for a younger slimmer *luckier* rabbit —
After a single film to a life in cartoon limbo:
Suspended animation.)

"Watch." Oswald pointed at the television again. "Now
you'll see something."

The screen blinked. Oswald the younger reappeared, this
time on board ship. The older Oswald jabbed his finger more
insistently. A blink and now young Oswald was in Mexico.

"Poor Papa!" the other Oswald shouted. "Poor Papa!"

But the picture was jumping around out of his control.
The on-screen Oswald mutated as he cavorted until his
complexion was almost completely white.

"Look at that. The sap. No scruples. He'd do anything to
stay in the movies. I said to Walt, *Walt*, I said, *he's no good.
He'll dirt on you.*"

He brought a slippered foot up and prodded the behind of
the person now fiddling with a solitary candle over the
obscured table.

"Isn't that what I said? *He'll split from you at the first smell of a bigger contract*. And he did, didn't he?"

Another grunted reply. Sam's eyes turned saucers. He took two hesitant steps forward.

"Well, who did you expect?" Oswald asked him.

Sam carried on towards the table. All light had leached from the room, save for that cast by the single birthday candle. Where the cake had been, though, there was now a clear glass dome. Sam peered inside and saw an entire city – houses and factories and ball-parks and malls – as if viewed from a plane. The face looking in from behind the candle flame was the face from the Disney Dream Diner, only nothing could have been further from it at this moment than a wink.

"Don't mind him," Oswald called to Sam. "That's all he ever does."

The candle went out and the room dropped into total darkness. (Someone somewhere in the black was sobbing.) Walt – because it *was* him – fumbled for a match.

"You see before you," Oswald said as the narrow light returned, "a disappointed man. His rabbit turned rat on him and his mouse became a monster."

Oswald mimicked Mickey's high-pitched voice.

"That right, Walt? Smile, smile, smile. Bombs and massacres and famines? No concern of ours. A smile and a cheery wave. Everything's dandy down on the farm."

Walt's shoulders hunched further. Oswald continued in his own voice.

"Had himself frozen. Thought he could return, like God on the last day, when his perfect world was complete. But the world's in a bigger mess than it ever was. He got it all ass-about, he gave them the wrong mouse. So he's stuck here with me, waiting."

"Waiting for what?" Sam asked.

"Not what, kid. *Who*."

A door opened at the far end of the room.

"Mortimer," Oswald whispered. "Mortimer was the mouse that should have been."

"But Mortimer . . . "

"Never existed? Sure he did. Walt thought him up. *And once you've thunk it, you never can dump it*. Don't they teach you anything any more? *Nothing* dies."

They were all three looking towards the door.

"Mort exists, all right. Mort's the guy we need."

The television screens twitched, the sobbing grew louder. The door at the end of the room remained open, gaping like an ache Sam felt right in his stomach.

A flight attendant shook his shoulder.

"Sir, we're ready to board the plane now."

*

It was all in the biographies. Oswald Mark 1; the rumours, which Sam had heard (and heard refuted) many times, that Walt had not been cremated when he died but had had his body preserved by cryogenesis. And Mortimer too, of course, Mickey's own Poor Papa, the mouse Walt's wife Lily rejected.

Easily explained.

Even so, elements of the dream came back to Sam sometimes in the moments before and after sleep, at the end of busy days or restless nights in Marne-la-Vallée. Half awake, once or twice, and aware that he was doing it, he even tried to reason away Oswald – the entire dream logic – using the evidence of his own eyes, the written record he kept of Euro Disney's construction. But the dream would not be dislodged for long. It came back to him the night of the trip up to Paris. Wearily, he marshalled his arguments as best he could. Paris, he was sure, the theme of the sacred heart, was conclusive proof that Walt had indeed got it right – you could impose an order on the city. He was too tired to contemplate the delinquent Son of Mickey, shooting up in the suburbs beyond Gare de l'Est. Too tired even to mention it.

A pattern was set that night, what didn't fit henceforth was left unsaid. And yet the more he felt he could not say the more the dream recurred, or the more Sam was drawn to re-enact it, until finally the night arrived when he was left without a word of any sort and he stood before Oswald, mute. Oswald took one look at him, exhausted from desperate hours of reading and writing, and came and put an arm round his shoulder. All of a sudden, Sam was crying.

"It's OK, kid."

They stood like that a long time together, Oswald's arm around Sam's shoulder, Walt, dejected, off to their right, clutching an inadequate light, all three looking towards the open door, aching for a fourth to appear.

And in the morning the heavy frost that had fallen in the night thawed turning the Euro Disney roads to swamp and Sam saw a man mired up to his belly holding a piece of the rainbow clear of the mud.

*

Sam arrived back in Paris that day desperate for guidance. The wind drove rain against the backs of his legs as he retraced his September steps, double-time, up the side of the Butte Montmartre. Now, though, there were few tourists in the shops and cafés of the place du Tertre and water lazed down the polythene sheets protecting the prints and menus displayed in the doorways. There were fewer still worshippers in the church of the Sacré-Coeur. Dribs and drabs. Sam took his place in the last row, rested his head a moment on the back of the seat in front, and only then allowed himself to raise his eyes. The Christ, as before, stretched his arms wide above the altar, crucified by the pain below him, each hurt, each wrong, another wrench on the golden cords of his heart. But there was something about the face which troubled Sam, a blandness, almost – indifference, he was tempted to say – and he knew then, of course, that he could return fifty years from now and no matter what enormities had befallen the world the heart would not have budged a single inch.

Over the next several hours he went into as many churches as he could find. (And in Paris that *was* many.) In each he discovered, whatever the outward differences, the same essential architecture of silence, in each he saw the same ·expression on the face of the crucified Christ. His pilgrimage ended in a church on the rue Saint-Martin. Christ was on his cross once more, two angels genuflecting in attendance. On the wall above this grouping was an explosion of gold and silver from which cherubs peeped forth, awed, while other bolder cherubs clung to golden shafts, reaching out their hands to the thorn-ringed head. The church was empty. Sam walked right up to the altar. The sides ascended in steps to the foot of the cross. This close, a crack was visible in the stone to the left of Christ's feet. Sam traced it round the back of the statue where it dipped and widened before tapering off once more. The plinth on which the cross stood was here almost split in two. The crack had been stuffed with old Mass cards and pages torn from newspapers. Looking up, Sam saw the heavy bolts which really held the Christ figure to the cross, saw too the electric cable tacked tight against the cross's side and other cables hugging the contours of the altar. Everywhere there were visible old round-pin sockets.

Special effects.

He heard a sound in the deserted church and glancing down saw his hands meet and part in a slow handclap.

Outside again, walking, *walking*, the street seemed a place of infinite refuge. Freed from his former quest, he bobbed along the sidewalks, head turned this way and that by the rain on the glasses of a passer-by – a patterned umbrella – an interesting hat – a fleeting smell of perfume or pipe smoke. So many people. His head whirled with their variousness, his mouth pulled a grin and held it till his chilled lips cracked and bled.

As the November night came down, he stopped on a narrow tongue of sidewalk where the rue Saint-Antoine forked into Rivoli. A single rudimentary carousel had somehow taken root here, its awning a species of giant patio umbrella of faded brown and orange, with pale pink strip-light spokes, its cars an unpeopled junkyard of metallic-painted automobiles, speedboats, and aircraft. Background music, a muffled Motown, struggled from a mono tape player suspended from a hook above the ticket booth. *Toora-lang-a-lang, toora-lang-lang*.

A sharp wind had got up. The ride owner stared out dolefully at the pedestrians hurrying by, clutching their coats closed. If I was in your shoes, his look seemed to say, I would do the same thing. Presently, though, a small child, asexual in anorak and pants, was led across the road by a woman old enough to be its grandmother. Mittens on lengths of coloured wool dangled three or four inches below the fingertips barely protruding from the cuffs of its coat. While the grandmother bought a ticket, the child wandered wide-eyed among the ride's gaudy cars, settling finally on a plum and silver helicopter and scrambling inside.

The wide eyes glanced back only once before the ride owner threw the switch and the helicopter pulled away, groaning, from the ground on its first, slow revolution. Empty cars passed Sam, gaining speed, rays of rose light spraying over their flanks. The rays converged on the curve of the helicopter's windshield as it came back into view side on, then sped away, as though from the child's forehead, as the helicopter swung round to face him. The child itself was unaware of this, mesmerised by the fact of movement, looking at its hands, its feet, at the ground left behind. Sam was enraptured. His heart kicked each time the helicopter returned, rising and falling on its hydraulic arm, rose-pink rays massing on the pale forehead and dispersing again, mittens waving in the slipstream. And Paris of a sudden was transmuted by this ludicrous apparatus, improbably located in a busy street, and all the grand schemes of emperors and presidents and kings were no grander than the fantasies of this small child, than the ambitions of the doleful man making his living behind the ticket booth – the pragmatism of the person who had stuffed a crack at the feet of Christ with waste paper. *Toora-lang-a-lang, toora-lang-lang.*

Crossing the Pont-Marie some little time later, Sam drew his wristwatch talisman from his pants' pocket and dropped it into the Seine. Oswald was right, Disney had wound up with the wrong mouse.

He had a drink to celebrate. Then another and another, bumping through the night from bar to bar.

A votre santé! Cheers! Here's mud in your eye.

Time turned liquid. He blinked his eyes shut and opened them on a vast café whose wall of sound was popped at intervals by champagne bottles being uncorked; blinked again and was in a low cellar, the clock, whose face was the sun and the moon entwined, showing a quarter after two. He tried to remember coming into this place – at moments through the night he had had the feeling he was not alone – but his thoughts dissolved and escaped his mind's grasp. He bought a drink all the same and determined to stay put.

In a recess about six or eight feet from the bottom of the

cellar stairs, a man in his early twenties, wearing a T-shirt and denim shorts, was singing accompanied on the piano by another, older man, as formal in dress as the singer was casual. On the wall behind them were shelves lined with files and ledgers. One, blue-bound, was marked *Ultra-Secret*. After two songs a third man, grey-bearded, but otherwise bald, entered the alcove and took down this blue file. It contained sheet music. He selected his song and handed it to the pianist, who massaged his fingers, familiarising himself with the score, then fluttered his hands over the keyboard, coaxing from it notes which filled out as the bearded singer's voice rose.

The bar counter itself occupied a cramped corner at an angle to the alcove piano. The bartender adjusted the lights according to the mood of the song. The available moods were high, low, and red. This was a red song. The audience sang along, swaying in their seats and on the packed triangular floor. They were, Sam now noticed, without exception, male. Again he had the feeling that he had been with somebody when he came in, but no one he fixed on looked in the least bit familiar. He had another drink. The music went from red to low to red again. And then all at once he spotted a face he was sure he recognised, moving along a passageway towards a harsher light beneath the stairs. Sam pushed through the tight wedge of bodies in pursuit and entered a rest-room containing on a scale with the remainder of the bar a single urinal, a corner wash-hand basin and, hard by, a narrow stall, the door of which was now closed. Sam waited for the man inside to finish. He was certain it had been the same face, the face that he had seen (the memory struggled to surface) the best part of a day ago now, tense beneath a rainbow on the road to Fantasyland. But he knew the second the door opened he had been mistaken. The man stood in the doorway straightening his belt buckle. The right side of his mouth curved up in a shy smile. Sam leant back against the wall and closed his eyes. He heard water running, then there was silence a moment, then a breath that was both sound and heat came close to his ear. He kept his eyes closed. There were words now, soft and warm, a hand on the wall between his arm and his side. He nodded. Lights danced in his head, red and rose-pink, plum and silver. The rest-room door opened, footsteps passed close by, urine flowed, the footsteps passed in the other direction, the door opened again and shut. The voice in his ear did not let up. The hand moved closer to his side, a knee was introduced between his knees, the thigh above it tensing where the muscles of his own thighs tapered. He nodded. From out of the swirl of lights a man appeared, not this man, the man whose hand was now brushing the hip of Sam's pants, but a man not unlike him, waving a rainbow like a standard. Behind him marched a host of men and women, struggling free from impossible loads, and in their hands they carried, on placards lashed to picks and shovels and brooms, the names of all the cities that ever were (. . . *and Babylon begat Seleucia and Seleucia begat Ctesiphon and Ctesiphon begat Baghdad . . .*), cities they had built, reclaiming them for their own. He saw again all that he had seen earlier that day, only this time he was in no doubt what it signified. The breathing in his ear quickened, but it was his own breathing he was hearing now, his own voice which burst out shouting: *Yes!*

*

A Trabant, its bodywork sprayed an abstract polychrome, was being pushed, in mid-morning autumn sunlight, by four men dressed in leather pants and waistcoats, towards the Fontaine des Innocents across the street from the Forum des Halles. One man sported a red kerchief knotted, pirate fashion, at the back of his head; all four wore shades. Sam was hunched in a doorway with a raggle-taggle bunch of kids he had picked up, or who perhaps had picked him up, somewhere around daybreak, sharing their morning bottle of vodka. Rock music (U2, one of the kids said) came from inside the Trabant, making of it a booming metal beat box, swamping everything else playing in the square. The four men – U2 doppelgängers – lounged against the car while other young men and women circulated leaflets bearing the love caution: *Achtung Baby*. A date was appended like a prophecy, 18 November. The music boomed, the doppelgängers posed, the raggle-taggle swigged vodka and boogied. Sam took his unsteady leave.

*

The Madeleine was obscured by a painted screen of the Madeleine. *Trompe l'oeil*. People were taking pictures, more people than had been taking pictures of any other attraction Sam had passed in his wanderings. They understood that it was even rarer than the real thing, this pink painted canvas. A flower-seller had had someone paint a life-size likeness of her and she sat beside this, before the screen in front of the Madeleine. She was doing twice the trade of the flower-sellers to the left and the right of her. An English tourist buying freesias for his wife was trying to explain with many ums and ahs that his wife too was Madeleine. The flower-seller smiled the smile of the professionally enchanted; Madeleine the wife moved her mouth in mute repetition of her husband's words, as though guarding him from embarrassment or harm.

A man had come to stand next to Sam, watching with him the three Madeleines, the Englishman, and the flower-seller beside herself with her brisk trade.

"It's something, you have to admit," he said, without turning his head, then after a pause in which he filled his lungs from an asthma inhaler, "Guillaume."

"Sam," Sam said.

"You need a place?"

Sam shook his head. Guillaume nodded his, lips pursed.

Later, in a café off rue Saint-Honoré, Sam saw him again. Guillaume saluted with his coffee cup across the room, as if congratulating Sam on having tracked him down. Sam reflected on his choice of this café out of all the many cafés in the district and almost felt inclined to congratulate himself. *Why this place?* A woman, Sam's age or younger, came in and sat with Guillaume, her back to Sam. Her brown-black hair was caught low with a white lace tie and the ends moved when she talked, brushing the cracked emblem of the two-tone New York Giants' jacket that sloped, several sizes too big, off her shoulders. Guillaume dipped his head closer to hers and she glanced over her shoulder at Sam. A bitter smell of chocolate from a crêpe cart parked on the sidewalk wafted in through a high slatted window. Sam put a hand to his temple, kneading the skin with his fingers. His entire body ached to sleep and yet a voice within him resisted, urging him to keep his eyes and ears open.

When he looked again, Guillaume and the woman were sitting side by side facing him. The woman, deadpan till then, smiled, with the unexpectedness of something being unhooked. Guillaume stood, took a boost from his inhaler, kissed the woman on both cheeks, and walked to the door. The woman remained a few minutes longer, smoking, her chin resting on the palm of her hand, then she too rose and left.

Sam's eyes watched her go (he even decided later that somewhere inside he had experienced a tinge of regret at her leaving), but his mind for the moment was elsewhere. Being two places at once, in fact, was fast becoming a norm for him. *Place* itself, if it came to that, no longer appeared unitary. The world was suddenly multiple and mosaic, teeming with possibility and chance. There was more than one way of looking at everything.

The smell of chocolate from the sidewalk was more bitter than ever. A waiter approached Sam's table and set down a saucer on which lay folded a piece of paper. Sam explained that he wasn't finished. The waiter shook his head. No, he said, the gentleman misunderstood. The piece of paper was from the young woman who had just left. Sam opened it, read the bare address written there, folded it and asked the waiter for another beer.

*

He had no book to guide him. He walked through a market where lychee skins littered the road, like discarded thumbstalls, and lambs hung inverted, stripped to their fleecy bobbysocks, a look in their eyes of final introspection.

He drank pale beer standing at the counter of a corner café. His neighbours, market workers and their customers, were all black. At length he addressed the man closest to him.

"Je cherche un Africain qui a travaillé à Euro Disney. Est-ce que vous en connaissez?"

The man at the bar raised a sceptical eyebrow.

"Bien des Africains y travaillent."

But *this* man, Sam began, and tried to explain about the mud and the rainbow. His neighbour raised his other eyebrow into an expression of no surprise, shrugged and continued talking to the person next to him.

At one point on his journey he broke his vow and entered a church, lured by the sound of a cello being played. At the rear of the huge organ lay a smaller chapel in which a wedding was in progress. The cellist played before the betrothed couple, solemn and timeless; a candle burned in a red glass on the altar behind the priest, brilliant in his white and gold robes. Tiredness came upon Sam like a weight in his soul. His legs weakened, he found a corner and sat in it. He felt if he closed his eyes now he would sleep for ever. At the last moment, though, he fought back, searching for a point to focus on. Behind the glass doors of the *sacristie de mariages*, a cream-coloured phone sat on a dark wooden table. The longer it didn't ring the more Sam was convinced it was going to. It seemed to him a reminder of another, more pressing world. Struggling to his feet, he ran down the nave and into the street, ran and ran until he had shaken his head free entirely of the cello's long lament.

Once in a while he took the folded paper from his pocket and read the address over to himself, then carried on walking, correcting an intuited wrong right turn with two lefts, dashing down passageways, backing out of blind alleys. As light was fading on the second afternoon, at the end of a covered hall with high bins along one wall, across a courtyard and up four flights, he found the Giants woman behind a treble-locked door, boiling coffee, two blue cups sitting on bright yellow saucers, waiting.

Her name was Aimée. She hooked her fingers on to the metal bed-head when they fucked, raising herself in the middle, as though balancing her cunt on the bow of bones curving inwards from her thighs. Lying on her stomach, she was broad-backed and wondrous, he thought he would never recover from so much skin. Her hair on the pillow was a black panic arrested by sleep, her hand on his shoulder was spread to steady her through the dreams which agitated her feet and buffeted the backs of her lilac eyelids. When she woke, her eyes themselves, an inch from his, were an unstable green, sunflowers curling their golden petals at the centre. Her scent was more pungent than any he would have believed till then attractive. He dipped his fingers in her warm-albumen mucus and trailed the tips along the dark hairs flecking the inside of her haunches. The second time they fucked he held on to the bed and shouted for her to stop – to go on – never to leave him. He took speed with her, face-down on the bed, working their way from the opposite ends of the line until their 50F proboscises touched. Their fucking now was furious and without climax, their conversation an endless, half-translated gabble. Beyond the shuttered windows, the sky went through its daily dramas of light and shade. Rain fell, the sun shone, night came and went, came and went.

Emerging from the bathroom into the murk of an early evening (he had no idea which), Sam saw Guillaume sitting at the foot of the bed. Guillaume rose and clasped Sam's hand.

"Aimée has told me. If you need any help, my friend . . ."

Guillaume winked and patted the side of his jacket. Sam glimpsed inside the butt of a revolver.

Aimée read a paperback novel, her eyes sweeping down the pages, jerking up and sweeping down again, without expression. Guillaume left.

"What did you say to him?" Sam asked.

Aimée frowned, trying to remember. Sam found his wallet on the floor by the bed, half his money taken. There was a bag of speed on the kitchenette worktop. He snorted the sulphate where it lay. Aimée continued to turn the pages of her book. Sam dressed, took a handful of pills from the vials on Aimée's side of the bed, and went out. It was two days before he found his way back and this time when the three locks were drawn a woman he had never seen before stood in Aimée's place.

"*Elle est partie*," she said. "Gone."

*

He checked into a hotel near Père Lachaise. He passed an entire afternoon exploring the cemetery's hilly *arrondissements* – now bohemian, now slum, now *grand-bourgeois*; follies succeeding shacks succeeding palaces and temples – searching for possible pointers. He used his room only for sleep and as the days passed slept less and less. He became well known in the streets and bars of Belleville and the quarter running down to the place de la Bastille. Wherever he stopped people would gather to hear him talk: *un vrai moulin à paroles*, a non-stop word-mill, pouring invective on purity and perfection in all their life-blighting guises. He criss-crossed the city from Saint-Denis to Gentilly, la Défense to Charenton-le-Pont (he calculated the journey time, on foot, to Croatia, to spread his message there), fuelling his walks, as he fuelled his thoughts, with ever greater quantities of amphetamine.

Mort was now ever-present in his mind, Papa Oswald made shambolic Mouse. Sam imagined a Disney world reconstituted around this ordinary Joe of a character and he accepted that it had fallen to him to prepare the way. But he had to choose the moment, and the manner, of his return with the maximum of care. He grew edgy in company and even when out on his own stopped often to glance in shop windows to ensure he wasn't being followed.

Spooked by a noise on the landing late one night, he settled his hotel bill and roamed the streets until dawn.

He spent that day at the window of his new hotel room in Château Rouge scrutinising the faces of the pedestrians passing below, a loaded gun (its provenance already obscure, but its presence somehow inevitable) dangling from his right hand. From then on he went out only under cover of darkness, seeking for the most part the cosmopolitan anonymity of Pigalle. Beneath the brashness, there was a frailty in the pursuit of its pleasures which appealed to him.

Mort, he was certain, would have stood, as he stood, hesitant before these doorways, dismayed and enthralled in equal measure.

Sitting in cramped auditoria he studied the shapes cast by the pale bodies on the stages and the screens (for white, black yellow or brown, all bodies were pale in Pigalle), as though by looking hard enough he could crack the code of their erotic semaphore. Each excursion held the expectation of a decisive enlightenment.

It was Friday night when he saw her. She and a friend were with three American soldiers in the back of what appeared to be a troop carrier. Sam arrived too late to discover what reason, if any, was given for them being there. Her friend was already undressed and straddling a GI. Another soldier was fondling the cheeks of her ass while the third, unbuttoning his fly, was fixing his gaze on Ilse Klein. The film was old but even so there was no mistaking the face. Sam was surprised for all of half a second before he understood that this was the point to which his odyssey had been leading.

The morning, though, found him indecisive. He had his principals but the prompt of plot still eluded him. All weekend he watched and waited.

And then, as day broke on Monday, Vukovar fell.

0520

Are you alive?

No.

Have you been dead for long?

How long is long?
Quite long, I suppose.

This century?

Yes.

Were you famous?   Were you a woman?

Yes. No.

A famous man.

Yes. Six.

That was a statement, not a question.

OK. Five.

Were you German?

No.

European?

No.

American?

Yes.

Were you involved in the war?

War? No.

You were in the movies, right?

Right.

A big romantic lead?

Wrong.

Were you ever in westerns?

No. I don't think so.
Not *cowboy* films like. . . No.

She's not John Wayne.

Let's see.
Were you around before Technicolor?

                    Yes.

                                        Were you in silent films?

                    Yes.

Ah: a silent comic?

                    Yes.

                                        Charlie Chaplin.

            Are you asking me?

                                                            Yes.

                    No.

Did you have a partner in your films?

                                        No.

                                        Buster Keaton?

                    No. Two left.

Wait. Think. Uh. . .

                                        Did you wear glasses?

Glasses?

No.

I was thinking of your man.
What do you call him?

Harold Lloyd?

No.

No, I was asking Ray if he was thinking of Harold Lloyd.

Yes, Harold Lloyd.

Last question. Guess.

Uh. . .   Am. . .

Harry Langdon.

Who?

Harry Langdon.

I have never even heard of Harry Langdon.

He was *famous*.

Perhaps, but I am not him.

Fatty Arbuckle!

Too late.

Is that who you are?

Yes, Fatty Arbuckle.

I'd never have guessed it.
Fatty Arbuckle.

What happens if you win?
Do you go again?

No, please, somebody else.

Ray?

Me? OK. Let me think.
Right, got one: go.

Are you alive?

No.

Were you a man?

Yes.

An Irishman?

No.

Ah, but be careful.
Raymond's from Belfast
British?

No. Not Irish,
not British,
not Ulsterish.

179

American?

Yes.

A dead American. A president?

No.

A rock star?

No.

You're an actor too?

Correct.

Did you die in the last ten years?

No.

Twenty?

No.

Were you also a silent movie star?

Yes.

You're Harold Lloyd?

No.

Harry . . . whatever his name is.

Langdon.

No.

But you are a comic?

Yes.

Charlie. . .

No: He said he did not die in the last twenty years.
Charlie Chaplin died in the last twenty years.

Point.

Did *you* have a partner?

No.

Buster Keaton?

No.

The cross-eyed one?

Turpin.

No.

It can't be Fatty Arbuckle.

Is that a question?

No.

You have three questions left.

Only three?

Two now.

That doesn't count.

It doesn't matter.
I can't think of any more.

Give up?

Yes.

No.
Wasn't the guy – the Keystone Kops –
the director, he was an actor too:
Mack Sennett?

No.

OK. I give up too.
Who are you?

Fatty Arbuckle.

Aw, *Ray*.

I said that.

But you didn't ask it.

Didn't I ask it?

No.

All right. Me now?

Yes.   Yes.

A minute.
Right.

Are you alive?

No.

Were you a man?

Yes.

An American?

Yes.

You lived this century?

Yes.

An actor?

Yes.

Fatty Arbuckle!   Fatty Arbuckle!

Yes.

For some minutes past the listening equipment which has been installed in and around Big Thunder Mountain has been picking up the weirdest conversation. It sounds like a game and it goes like this:

"Are you alive?"

"No."

"Are you Fatty Arbuckle?"

"Yes."

And that's it. The hostages and their captor, in combination and in turn.

(Two voices) "Are you alive?"

(One voice) "No."

(Two voices) "Are you Fatty Arbuckle?"

(One voice) "Yes."

Time after time after time. But, get this, they are all three laughing. Like beer buddies. Like nutcases.

Gary turns to the psychiatrist standing at his side.

"Has he got them *all* on that stuff?"

"*Stockholm Syndrome*," the psychiatrist says, "an extreme example," and Gary reflects that psychiatrists as a profession are singularly unable to share a joke.

He brings the field glasses to his eyes and for what he

reckons must be the thousandth time tonight trains them across the mud on Big Thunder Mountain, peering into its orifices. The orifices continue to call back to him over the drone of the doctor's diagnosis.

Fatty Arbuckle
Fatty Arbuckle
Fatty Arbuckle.

The end begins at 0600.

Crash. Sam hits a new dramatic low. Ilse and Raymond are aware of it first as a stillness between them protracted to the point where *they* can endure it no longer and their stiff limbs start despite them to fidget.

"Sam? Sam? Is everything all right?"

Sam's shoulders rise and fall at last under the blanket (which stinks by now, like capital *s*), but the sigh that accompanies the movement is the sigh of a person four times his age. Octogenarily he gripes and grumbles: his eyes hurt, his ears and nose hurt; his *teeth* hurt.

"Where the fuck is Mort? I'm getting tired of waiting."

Right on cue, Gary's voice is there, the urgency of his response belying the calm he strives to impart.

"You know, Sam, I think we're close to sorting something out here. Things are really starting to move. They really are. You ask me, the two of us are going to be able to talk this out just fine."

But Sam is tired of talking too.

"I listen to your words," he tells Gary, "but they don't *say* anything."

He is suddenly *very* hungry. He is sure Ilse and Raymond

must be as well. He wants to arrange for food to be sent in.

Gary tells him that *that's* talking. He only has to say the word and the food will be there. But first things first.

"No, food first," Sam says. "Food *now*."

"OK, now," Gary says, "but I have a doctor here would like to take a look at the hostages."

It is policy on Gary's part to remind Sam at every opportunity that he has hostages, that he is, therefore, a kidnapper, a felon.

Sam tells him that he and the doctor can go fuck themselves. There is only one person getting in this mountain, besides the person bringing the pizzas (for *pizzas* the food has now in Sam's mind very definitely become), and Gary knows well enough who that is. Gary hums and haws. Well, it's like this, his instructions were that food was permissible, but only so long as a doctor was let in to see the hostages. He'll have to go away and check again. Sam is fuming. *Go and check?* He'll do no such thing. Check with who? What is this all of a sudden?

"Come on, Sam," Gary says. "You know the way this works. You know everything has to be authorised from up above before I can OK it."

The gun in Sam's right hand makes an unequivocal click.

"I have been sitting here for eleven hours and what have I asked you for? A bucket to piss in, that's all. I have been *so* reasonable. I could have asked to talk to the media. I could have demanded *cameras*. How would that have looked, Gary? Big Thunder Mountain blowing its top on prime-time."

Gary agrees (he is thinking *Dog Day Afternoon*): "You could have, Sam." And straight away realises he has made a mistake. For a few vital seconds he is at a loss for words.

"I want to talk to the media," Sam says. "I want cameras."

"One thing at a time, one thing at a time," Gary says, desperate to recover the lost ground. "The food. You must all be pretty ravenous in there."

But just as suddenly as the desire to eat came on Sam it leaves him again.

"Not food, cameras. If Mort doesn't get through in the next hour, I want . . . *CNN* here to tell them how I've been left with no alternative but to blow up the mountain."

(Sam has to keep reminding himself that there is no bomb, that the backpack contains only auto batteries and a bunch of wires. And yet he is almost inclined to let himself believe in the bomb's existence, since the people out there cannot know he doesn't have one, or even if they suspect it, cannot afford to take the risk. Imagine, after all, Big Thunder Mountain blowing its top, prime-time or no prime-time.)

Raymond, who, like Ilse, has been listening to this exchange as though somehow outside of it (they were *laughing and joking* with this man not fifteen minutes ago) now finds a gun barrel jammed under his chin.

"He's serious!" he shouts to Gary – to anyone beyond the mountain walls with ears to hear. "He'll kill us."

"Now wait, Sam."

There is a distinct hardening in Gary's tone.

"You're serious, I'm serious, everybody's serious. But you're not a fucking idiot, *I'm* not a fucking idiot. You *know* the way these things work." (He thinks for a moment to ask Sam has *he* seen *Dog Day Afternoon*.) "You get nothing without we get something in return. That's the height of it."

The ante has been upped. A minute ago Gary might have settled for allowing food in exchange for the doctor. But cameras?

"Let . . . *Ilse* go and we can really start to do business."

(Ilse is almost stung by this to protest: *Of course, Ilse is a woman, let her go first, obviously*. But Sam, as always, has the radio.)

"Well, look at it another way, Gary. I get nothing and you get Ilse – and Ray – dead. How's *that* for height? Some negotiator you'd be."

He feels obliged at this juncture to turn to Raymond and Ilse and tell them that if they die it will not be his fault. They know by now the kind of person he is, but they have to see that this is out of his hands. He did not choose to come here and he cannot simply leave again without fulfilling the task which was set him. It is much too serious for that. The world cannot just be left to drift along as it is, tearing itself apart, wasting people's lives.

"And what is this if it is not waste?"

Ilse it is who asks the question, though it is not her own life she is thinking of.

Sam is appalled.

"I can't believe you said that, Ilse."

He is shouting. Ilse and Raymond have rarely heard him so angry tonight.

"After all that we have talked about. I really cannot believe you said that."

Ilse shrugs off the attack.

"I only meant that you have done so much already to come this far. I will not forget, Raymond, I am sure, will not forget. If anyone asks me I will tell them everything you told us. And I will tell them how you convinced me, how I came to agree with what you were doing."

"Yes," Raymond says. "We'll go to the television and the newspapers."

Sam does not even try to keep the contempt out of his voice.

"You really do have no idea, do you? I am not doing this for you, I am doing this *because* of you. Fuck-ups."

And with that he seems to shut himself off from them completely. Ilse and Raymond are thrown once more into the confusion of several hours before with only the blanket that binds them to cling to. More words are exchanged between Gary and Sam. Ilse and Raymond, such is their despondency, are unable to grasp a single one of them distinctly, though the general air of impasse is unmistakable. The radio contact breaks down again. Minutes pass without a word of any sort being spoken. Dreadful minutes. The silence appears irrevocable.

And then Raymond, surprising even himself, summons what is left to him of courage and asks to be allowed to send a message to his daughter. Sam refuses to begin with, but when the request is made a second time, and with more force, he (not unconscious of the theatrics of the gesture) gives his assent. He gets Gary on the radio and tells him to have someone standing by to take this down.

"It's all yours, Ray."

The lights, the realisation of audience, have Raymond for an instant tongue-tied. He begins, eventually, by telling Stephie he doesn't know where to begin. It will be hard for her to come to terms with the loss of her father in this way (though he understands she has had to live with the loss of him, in one form or another, all her life), but she is not to feel bitterness towards the man who has killed him. This will be hard for her to come to terms with too, but he thinks, in fact, he may have been a party to his own death, because long ago he increased the amount of hatred and division in the world. He went out one night with the intention of killing a man, a man he did not even know, had never even seen. He was young then but that was no excuse. The young above all must not kill, or the killing will never cease.

(Sam *nods* at this.)

After that he says pretty much what you would expect a man about to die to say to his daughter. He wishes he had been a better father to her, he wishes he had had the chance to see her grow up, he hopes she works hard, does not make the same mistakes he has made, he hopes above all she will be happy.

Well, all right, what would *you* say?

As always with Stephie, though, Raymond is left feeling he ought to have said something more, or nothing at all. She knows so little of him, and that little by way of others, that he wants her to have one memory that could only have come from him, to share with her something that he has never before shared with anyone, not even tonight when he has shared so much else.

"Is that it?" Gary asks.

Raymond is aware that time is running out, but he will not be rushed. He is thinking of the years after his release from prison, before he left Belfast. He was friendly for a time then, he tells Stephie (tells, incidentally, all of Frontierland, the whole tense assembly of police and soldiers and medics and fire-fighters and Euro Disney officials and their US embassy counterparts), friendly with a man by the name of Ferguson. *Samuel* Ferguson, oddly enough, given the name of the man who is holding him here, and given too that this man Ferguson was a Roman Catholic. (And no sooner has he said this than he apologises that his daughter has grown up in a place where such store is set by names.) Samuel had an aunt lived in Omeath, immediately to the south of the Irish border. The border, in fact, ran up the middle of Carlingford Lough at the foot of the aunt's garden. Samuel had invited Raymond down to stay one weekend and the two men had stood in the garden after the drive from Belfast, drinking beer, looking across into the North (which at that point was due east) to Narrowwater, where some years before the IRA had killed almost a score of paratroopers in an ambush. As they were talking, trying to reconcile the peacefulness of the scene with the carnage of that other day, they noticed that the tide had started to go out, and over the next few hours, coming and going in and out of the house, they watched without comment the water recede further and further towards the mouth of the lough until at the exact same moment they turned and looked at each other and began to laugh, *where had the border gone now?*

You had to be there, of course, but though it wasn't much of a joke in the retelling Raymond wanted Stephie to know how often that moment had come back to him in the years since – how often he had actively called it to mind. Because the more he had laughed about it the more he realised it was himself in part he was laughing at.

(At the age of thirty, Samuel Ferguson married a Protestant called Mary Murphy, a part-time private in the UDR. When Samuel next visited his aunt, alone, a month after the wedding, someone attached a booby-trap bomb to the underside of his car. It failed to explode and fell off in a garage forecourt just beyond Newry. The following month someone else called at Samuel's house in Belfast to shoot him, but he and his wife were out, so the someone else shot Samuel's dog instead for failing to recognise the legitimate armed representatives of the republican struggle and barking. A month after that again, Samuel Ferguson was knocked down and killed while crossing the street to a Chinese take-away. Stephie was to watch out for that too. They were lunatics, you know, Belfast drivers.)

Ilse Klein has no messages to send. Her parents are themselves dead and her brother will hear of her death, if die she does, and make of its circumstances what he will. Ilse's brother is a clever man, a famous man in Germany, a lawyer who in his time has defended many of those known as the Red Army Faction. You would have seen him perhaps on television, fourteen years ago now, outside Stammheim Prison, pointing an accusing finger – mocking the police with a Nazi salute – the morning after Andreas Baader, Jan-Carl Raspe and Gudrun Ensslin were found dead in their cells.

Konrad will have his own ideas about Sam's actions. As you would expect of a man who has explained to his own satisfaction how a group dedicated to exposing the fascism latent in the capitalist state should end up murdering Jews, he is a past master at making things fit. His sister, Ilse, fits into the category of faint-hearts and turncoats. She betrayed herself and the revolution, whoring her body for the cameras. And it is the greatest betrayal of all to suggest as Ilse suggested last time they spoke, long before Stammheim, that it was the revolution itself which had turned traitor.

*

In Maine, where it is now twenty minutes after midnight, Sam's parents, Holly and Tom, are informed that their son has declined the invitation to speak to them direct. A phone line has been kept open through the night between their harbour home and Marne-la-Vallée, though the psychiatrist assigned to the case has deemed it unwise before now to use it. Behind the house, out of sight of the street, waits a car which will drive them on a prearranged signal to a US Air Force base where a plane too waits, fuelled for a flight to France.

They had been expected to dinner earlier at a friend's house, but cancelled as soon as they were contacted at the gallery late yesterday afternoon and told to stand by for news of their son. The past two weeks, since Sam's disappearance from Euro Disney, have been an appalling strain. It would have been hard to imagine any outcome short of his death (and, throughout, they were both convinced that somewhere he was still alive) which would have been more intolerable than that period of not-knowing. But they had not for a minute reckoned on anything like this. They can scarcely credit that it is their son talking in the encrypted reports faxed through to their kitchen from the Magic Kingdom at thirty-minute intervals and re-rendered verbatim by the secret service agent who sits at the family table sipping iced tomato juice.

Tom separates and musses his beard (sparser these days than it was when he and Holly first crossed the continent to New Dawnland; sparser, but just as red), enunciating words and phrases, hoping for some flash of recognition, but what isn't wholly alien to him – *Mort* for Christ's sake? – merely warps on his tongue, so that even the shared past becomes suspect and he is left wondering did they ever know their son at all, or he them. (I mean, hadn't they always taught him, *Speed Kills?*)

The fax breaks aside, there is silence in the house and then there is more silence. The television is on but soundless. Yellow ribbons add their own mute taunt. The call that feels as though it will never come never comes. Nor can Holly and Tom call out to friends for support, because none of this as yet, officially speaking, is happening. They don't talk to each other (in truth, they barely look at each other) because what is there to say? Apart from what they have said time and again this past fortnight, that there comes a moment when parents have to accept, for their own sanity, that they are not responsible for the actions of their children.

*

"What can they possibly say to me?" Sam wants to know. "They thought all it was about was avoiding LA and not eating junk food. They kept themselves pure by building a little fort at the water's edge and made the world safe for summer tourists. They think they are, but they are no better than these people beside me. They are not the *equal* of these people beside me."

Holly and Tom reading this shake their heads.

The psychiatrist next to Gary shakes his head. Such a level of caprice from the kidnapper was to be feared. One minute the hostages are his sworn enemies, the next they are the very salt of the earth. The amphetamine abuser is the least predictable of characters – especially at this stage of the cycle. Worse, there exists now a very real danger that his own body might soon, as it were, be at war with itself – right hand literally not knowing what the left is doing – and there will be no telling then how he might react.

He informs Gary that they are approaching a critical moment.

Day is beginning to break, if break is not too energetic a word for that slow dilution taking place at the edge of darkness, as though the sky, having strained all night for a perfect pitch black, has overreached itself, revealing its undercoat of striated slate and clay, the raw materials of morning.

Gary talks to some people Stateside, listens a time, tight-lipped, then hands over control to the police and army chiefs with him on the ground. The chiefs confer briefly before giving the go-ahead to the party standing by at the mouth of the tunnel up to Big Thunder Mountain and directing the snipers to move into position.

*

Sam places one arm around each of his companion's necks and hauls them to him, hoarse-whispers in their ears.

"It will be all right. Whether they want him to or not, he *is* going to come."

They are digging mass graves in the fields outside Vukovar. In a short while the Serb militias will begin emptying the hospital, clinically: bed by bed, stretcher by stretcher, shot by shot. An act which will come with repetition to be termed (language wrung through an ideological mangle) cleansing. Already the Slavonian capital Osijek, twenty miles to the north-west, is coming under renewed shelling. There are one hundred and forty thousand people there to classify and process. And then there is Dubrovnik, on the Adriatic coast. And then there is Bosnia.

"Damn Vukovar," a woman, fleeing, is heard to shout. "Damn my whole life."

*

In Belfast, where Mickey Mouse and Donald Duck are due to appear later in the week to switch on the Christmas tree lights, a woman lies in bed unable to sleep for thinking about condoms. She has practised all day, getting used to having one inside her (she can almost recall the feeling now if she presses her legs tight together), getting used to moving around the house, going to the shops, climbing on and off buses, with it secure in her vagina. In fact, it is the weight, not the sheath itself, that she has most difficulty accustoming herself to. (This *is* 1991, the word of the Church long ago ceased to be read as writ.) She had never expected a mere ounce to have such definite substance.

Six of these condoms can carry enough Semtex to make a very effective bomb; effective enough when it explodes – as one will this coming Sunday in the C Wing dining hall of Crumlin Road prison – to kill a man outright and injure many more.

The aim of a bomb in a prison dining hall, the woman understands, is to force the demand for segregation between loyalist and republican prisoners.

The territorial war must be carried on on all fronts. What you have you hold, even if all you are left holding in the end is rubble.

*

In Los Angeles, as in cities large and small throughout the USA, narcocops of the DEA are cleaning up the streets, shaking down suspected drug dealers (to wit, any non-Anglo youth abroad on the night-time streets), confiscating, as is their federal right, money, watches, rings, even cars; presumed proceeds of unproven felonies. The war on drugs is escalating. Helicopters police the skies, whole neighbourhoods are placed under snap curfews. Fault lines, more dangerous than the geological, grow daily more apparent. Actual possession carries a possible five-to-fifteen in one of the city's ever-expanding, and soon-to-be sky-scraping, penitentiaries. The prison population is shooting up, here and elsewhere. Britain, following the American lead, presses ahead with jail privatisation. Drugs are much on the government's mind there too. In Manchester, where drug gangs, LA-style, the horrified tabloids report, battle for territory round the clock (work is not a distraction, work being the one commodity permanently in short supply), crack cocaine is being sold behind the Salisbury bar by Oxford Road station, on the spot where the inventor of the computer – harbinger of the city's industrial decline – was once arrested for homosexual solicitation. (He subsequently committed suicide. Drug overdose, of course. Coincidence is the city's fourth dimension. Coincidences are pearls we collect and string together.) Jails might yet be for the building trade in recession what malls were in time of growth, the new cathedrals.

You get the city you project. A Narcopolis for the Narcopolice to patrol.

Nat Stanley, shod and clad for manual labour, kneels on the floor of his eight by twelve two-bunk room for the third time already this morning talking to his friend Jesus. He asks the Saviour's blessing on all his friends here at Euro Disney and especially on his good friend Raymond Black. He asks that the Lord will lift from Raymond's shoulders whatever terrible burden it is he carries. He prays that Raymond will see at last, as Nat himself has seen, the True Light of Christ's Love.

He asks – in passing you understand – that the Lord will grant his servant, Nat, a place working inside Big Thunder Mountain again today, for the Lord knows of his kidney problems (as he knows the ins and outs of the least of his creatures, Praise be) and today looks set to be very damp and cold.

*

Quigley tells Mullan your man Inspector Dick never came back to the monastery last night. Mullan's hand, clutching a wet face cloth, pauses in mid-revolution on his stubbly head. They look at each other in the wash-room mirror, who never look at anyone straight unless they mean to stare them out (for eye-to-eye is not unmanly at this remove).

"Are you sure?" Mullan asks.

His stomach, reflected, is an archipelago of mustard bruises, the three-week-old traces of the love-bites he was awarded, the departing hero, the night before he left Belfast for France.

Quigley nods: "Sure."

Mullan shrouds his face with the cloth, breathes in, imprinting it with his features, then out, letting it peel over his nose and slowly down his chin.

He grins, Quigley too.

"*Fucking harden him!*"

*

Pepe has been on the go since half-past five. The dashboard of his van is hot to touch, but the warmth from the heater extends no further than the steering wheel so that only his hands and feet have any feeling in them. Rachid huddles in the seat beside him, sunk in a vast but inadequate quilted anorak. A Russian soldier's winter cap falls almost over his eyes. For a famous week at the end of October a stall was established in a field on the perimeter of the Magic Kingdom, selling the cast-off uniforms of Eastern Bloc armies. Hundreds upon hundreds of coats and hats and pairs of trousers and pairs of boots: surplus on a superpower scale. The flaps of the cap hide the earphones of the Taiwanese walkman which Rachid listens to (bought from a stall in another field in mid-September) and from which Moroccan music leaks, like an overheard dream of home.

Pepe drives carefully on the uneven road. As always at this time of the morning, he is carrying several hundred eggs in the back of his van. As always at this time of the morning, his thoughts turn to Ilse Klein. In all the months she has worked for him she has never taken a day off, has never been so much as a minute late arriving at the canteen. Without his quite realising it, Pepe has come depend on her. Totally. It has been in his mind for some weeks now to invite her to dinner one Sunday at the house he rents in the village of Moulignon. He is, though, if the truth be known, a little in awe of her. He has seen, left lying in the kitchens, the books that she reads, he suspects that in her life before Disney she was something more than a mere canteen assistant. All the more reason then to talk to her soon – today. Pepe has plans, plans which involve Ilse Klein. He aims to leave the Singer canteen and go into business for himself. He looks in the newspapers and everywhere he sees change, empires collapsing, new countries appearing. Europe is a building site, and where people build, of necessity they eat.

*

Kent Weinberger eats breakfast in the French style, croissants and *café crème*. From a fruit bowl on the table he eats a peach and then a pear, from the ice-box he eats a slice of mirabelle pie. But still his spirits refuse to be lifted.

He drinks another bowl of coffee, thinks.

In Meaux last night to see a movie he bumped into Bob Bardon, an Imagineer friend, just returned from a meeting in Paris, who claimed he had sighted Sam earlier in the day along the road from Esbly. Kent told him that was impossible, Sam was still on sick-leave (for thus has his absence, to the general disbelief, been explained); Bob, though, was adamant. He was in a cab being driven to the train station and looking out the window had seen Sam walking in the opposite direction on the far side of the road.

"Boy was he travelling. Talk about *jet*-boots!"

Kent sat for an hour after getting back to the apartment, having first searched for and failed to find any sign of his house-mate, then telephoned the embassy. They thanked him for his prompt action, said they would look into the matter in the morning, advised him to go to bed. Kent sat a half-hour longer, then did as advised. His eyes, though, defied the command to close. After another hour and a half, he got up again.

He finishes his coffee, watching the clock – as he has watched it at intervals throughout the night – tell off the seconds. With each one, his frown grows deeper, and the thought occurs to him that there is only so much time, then no more.

Tut, tut, tut.

0658

At Big Thunder Mountain the generators fall silent.

"Just before seven o'clock, the beams stopped criss-crossing the chamber, then a single light came on, very bright, down the track, where it dipped underground, and footsteps started up the tunnel . . . "

"The first thing any of us saw was the tops of the ears . . . "

"Sam's eyes opened like big flowers."

" . . . *Mouse* ears, then the rest of the head . . . "

"The shadow reached almost to our feet: the light was at its back, shining right in our faces."

"But you could see . . . "

"Sam let go of the ends of the blanket and stood up shielding his eyes."

"Then the light dimmed and suddenly the shadow disappeared and there was just this little Mouse-man, I guess you'd call him, his face . . . "

" 'What the hell time is this to be getting me up at?' he asked Sam."

"Sam turned to us, and the look on his face was like *Can you believe this?*"

"He moved down on to the track, keeping us covered with the gun. There was just that one weak light now. There were sounds – people moving – in the shadows all around us."

"But the bag, they were still afraid . . ."

"Sam was edging forward. 'Is it really you?' he said. And the Mouse – he was a fat guy . . . "

"Yes, and his face . . . "

" . . . in an old, what-d'you-call-it, bowling shirt. He looked down at himself and lifted his hands as if to say . . ."

" . . . you could see, like lines, no, not lines . . . "

" 'If I'm not me I don't know who I am.' "

" . . . *scars.*"

"He reached into his hip pocket and spilt some, um . . ."

"Lotto tickets,"

"and then pulled out this long string of – there must have been forty"

"or fifty – "

"photographs. 'Who are they?' Sam asked."

"The Mouse-man looked at them as though he had forgotten he had taken them out."

" 'Kids,' he said. 'And their kids.' "

"And Sam said something like: 'Jeez, there's enough of them.' And the Mouse said, 'Ah, well . . . ' "

"No, first he said, 'Listen, call me Mort.' Straight out: 'Call me Mort.' "

"Right, and then he folded the pictures away. 'Well, you know,' he said. 'Kids: some got on . . .' "

" ' . . . some got eaten . . . ' "

" ' . . . some got by.' "

"Sam let his gun arm fall to his side."

"And suddenly . . . "

" – His back was to us – "

" . . . there were hands covering our mouths, grabbing our arms and legs . . ."

" . . . at the same moment that the Mouse . . . "

"I was trying to bite the hand over my mouth, I wanted to shout, 'Sam, look at his scars!' "

" . . . opened *his* arms."

"Sam swayed on his heels a little and then kind of . . . "

" . . . lurched forward . . . "

" . . . *stumbled*."

"The Mort guy jerked back a second, thinking, maybe, the bag . . . "

" . . . the bag was on the track between them . . . "

" . . . and then there was a . . . "

" – only one – "

" . . . shot."

"Sam spun."

"And spun."

"And spun."

"And there were police – soldiers maybe – rushing in from all sides."

"I was screaming. There was a hole in Sam's forehead. He straightened a moment, then toppled."

"And the Mouse, Mort . . . "

"Only it wasn't Mort. You could see . . . "

" . . . caught him."

" . . . the scars. It was only Mickey with his face all messed up to look older."

Walter Elias Disney started life on a farm outside of Marceline, Missouri
– a middling town in the Middle America whose values he made a fortune animating –
ended it making plans to build the city of tomorrow
Walter Elias, known to the world as plain Walt Disney, loved the little things in life like mice and ducks and chipmunks and his miniature private railway, loved the little things and thought big
He dreamed a kingdom in the Californian orange groves (the kingdom-dreamer's paradise), a home for his favourite son, the god-king of his cartoon empire, M-I-C K-E-Y . . .
But the moneychangers and the sellers of doves crowded at its gates and he went and dreamt another one twice the size of all Manhattan down near the town of Kissimee, Florida, where long years before his parents swapped their marriage vows
Only this time he bought control of all the land round about and did a deal with the State authorities which gave him the right to raise his own police force and set his own laws and gave them from that day forward no right to enter the territory without absolute Disney say-so

He toyed with the idea of housing his workers in an artificial mountain, where the air too was free from outside taint, then abandoned that and pressed ahead with an even more audacious dream

EPCOT

he said would be "a planned, controlled community" a model city for a world where cities were getting out of control (his friend Ray Bradbury who had a few ideas of his own about the city of tomorrow told him once he ought to run for mayor of LA

Ray, he said, or so the story goes, why should I run for mayor when I'm already king?)

EPCOT

he said would have no slums and no landowners and therefore no voting control (other than his own) and though he died long before building had begun the rumour was he had himself put on ice, frozen against the day when a cure could be found for all his ills and he would return like the risen urban saviour to his ideal city

Only the ideal city was never built

Without his overseeing eye EPCOT was translated into Interworld (echoing, too closely for some, the cryogenic hiatus in which he was reputedly suspended) then hastily translated back, though not far enough to meet his original expectations, so that it was said that even the final version would have had him turning in his grave

Always supposing he had a grave to turn in

Which is as may be, but the germ of the dream that first took root in the orange groves of Anaheim – of creating not just static pleasure parks but living breathing growing entities – the germ of that dream was never let die, but was nurtured there and in Florida and eventually transplanted across the sea first in Tokyo then in Paris, France

Two more Magic Kingdoms, virtual simulacra of the American originals
(Two more mini Marcelines at their Main Street hearts)
Two more Haunted Mansions
Two more fairy-tale castles
Two more Big Thunder Mountain rides, their narrow-gauge tracks like strips of film awaiting the animating imprint of trains, the *action* of passing lives.

Ilse Klein and Raymond Black visit Euro Disney as often as they can afford. They have ridden the Big Thunder Mountain ride tens of times, looking out in the whirl and hurtle for the ledge where they sat through the night with Sam, waiting for Mort. The whole thing is over so fast, though, they never can agree on the exact spot. They bicker about it as soon as they are off and have to queue to go back round again, and so it carries on until their day runs out. But still they can't agree on where it was they sat. Or even when. They are so far gone now, their lives are folding over on themselves. They live in a world of illusions and shades; they make up stories neither of them believes; they have dreams and visions and flashbacks; they say hi to people they have never met; they search one another's faces sometimes and wonder who they are. They think though there was a time – a week perhaps, a day, or maybe just a morning – when they looked at each other with clear heads and clear eyes and understood.

Acknowledgements

The extract from *Morning Prayer* (p. 5) is courtesy of the BBC and Professor Haddon Wilmer.

The passage relating to Jean de Berry on pp. 81-3 is my own rendition of the account of the duke's life in Barbara Tuchman's *A Distant Mirror*.

I would like to thank the Authors' Foundation for their financial assistance, also the following universities (and their respective Arts Councils) for employing me as writer in residence during the researching and writing of this novel: the University of East Anglia, University College Cork, Queen's University Belfast.

Thanks, too, to the friends who at various stages read and commented on the manuscript: Marc O'Day, Colette Fagan, Damian Smyth, Robert Wilson, Martha Perkins; and to Ali FitzGibbon, for reading it, helping frame the Twenty Questions, and answering yes to the one that really mattered.